HOPE IS BORN

AN ADVENT DEVOTIONAL
BJ LAWSON

ABOUT THE AUTHOR

BJ Lawson is an international writer, speaker and Bible teacher.
Her background is in teaching people how to study the Bible, and training
others how to make disciples -- who make disciples. She is passionate about
seeing others engage Jesus through Bible study in a way that keeps Jesus at the
core of every aspect of their lives with the goal of making Him known
to everyone they encounter.

TABLE OF CONTENTS

INTRODUCTION

I love Christmas! It's my very favorite time of year! I love everything about it... decorating the house, and of course, the tree, searching for and finding gifts for those special people in my life, singing, celebrating, visiting, the smells, the sounds and, of course, family!

At the center of all of this is the reason we celebrate, the birth of a baby, the first coming of the Lord Jesus Christ.

Over the years I have found the busyness of the season slowly encroaching on my time of reflection. I was going through the motions of celebrating but began to realize I had lost the childlike wonder of Christmas. (Not the wonder of Rudolf with his shiny red nose, or the magical sleigh delivering packages to every girl and boy in the world in one night, nor Santa who is the head of this operation.) But the wonder of a baby born to a virgin, a star that directs men from another country to the home the child lives in, angels announcing the baby's arrival to shepherds in the fields, a baby who had been talked about for hundreds of years who isn't simply an ordinary baby but is extraordinary because He is fully God. The difference between the two stories is that one is truth and one is fantasy. One impacts hearts and minds for a season, the other for eternity.

I found a need for centering, which is when I first incorporated Advent readings into my celebration. Immediately I fell in love with daily Advent readings! They help keep me focused on Jesus Christ, and the wonder of it all. They opened my eyes of understanding to God's glorious plan, which He had from the very beginning of time, and the dots began to connect. As I read about the Wise Men I had so many questions like, How, being from Babylon, did they know there would be a baby born? Why would God reveal this to Gentiles? Why did the religious leaders not seek Him? Many more questions danced around in my head. When the Wise Men arrived at the home of this extraordinary child, they fell on their knees, undone, and worshiped Him. I found myself doing the same, and I realized the wonder had returned!

For many years my husband and I have taken groups to Israel on study tours. We tour and teach on many of the major sights as well as a few more obscure ones. It's one of our favorite things to do. We love to see the excitement on faces as they begin to really grasp where they are, when they begin to connect the dots of events and places they had only read about, and are now coming alive complete with sights, sounds and smells!

This year as I stood in Bethlehem, I looked at it with very different eyes, eyes of understanding. It still is a very insignificant town, small in size, just about five miles from Jerusalem. The landscape has changed since that night nearly 2,000 years ago, when shepherds kept watch over their flocks in the fields. The setting is still serene, the stars at night, still brilliant, shine through the clear desert sky. Yet at the same time pilgrims from around the world flock there in order to see where the Christ child was born. I couldn't help being curious about whether or not any of those visitors really understood the wonder of it all.

I challenge you to not be distracted by all things shiny, parties and gift buying, so as to miss the real reason we celebrate! Take time each day to recalibrate, intentionally making room for Jesus by meditating on the Scriptures and pondering the wonder of Christmas! At the end of the Daily Devotionals there is a section called **Daily Bible reading** and one labeled Something to Think About. Do not simply skim through them. In order to get the most out of each devotional and to grow in your walk with the Lord, read each section thoroughly and follow the instructions given. Each day record in the journal pages provided, what the Lord revealed to you during this time. At the end of the Advent season write in the pages those details you may have missed in years past, what captivated your heart this year, and how this year impacts the way you will celebrate in years to come!

As the story unfolds before you, may it recapture your heart, connect the dots and restore that childlike, hope filled wonder of Christmas!

WHAT IS ADVENT?

Advent is what we call the season leading up to Christmas.

Since before Creation, God had a plan. From the fall of man God prepared His people for the coming of His Son, our hope. We are a people of promise. We celebrate the realization of God's promises of rescue and redemption at Christmas.

For four weeks, we step back and remember the thousands of years God's people were anticipating and longing to be rescued, for the coming of God's salvation plan, Jesus. That's what advent means, "coming" or "arrival." They were waiting but had no idea who the rescuer was or when he would come on the scene.

The entire season is centered on:

- The celebration of the birth of Jesus the Christ in His First Advent.
- The anticipation of the return of Christ the King in His Second Advent.

Advent is much more than simply marking a 2,000-year-old event in history. Advent is a season of preparation. Not only is Advent about preparing to celebrate the first coming of Christ as the Savior, but it's also about preparing for Christ's second coming as Judge. During Advent we are reminded that the Christmas story began thousands of years before the birth of Jesus, with the people of Israel. During the season of Advent we are also reminded that the Christmas story is not over. Jesus will return.

Acknowledging both provides a basis for Kingdom living which comes from a profound sense that we live "between the times" and are called to be faithful stewards of what is entrusted to us as God's people. So, as the church celebrates the birth of Christ, and anticipates His soon coming return, it also confesses its own responsibility as a people commissioned to bring the gospel message to the world, living life loving the Lord your God with all your heart and loving your neighbor as yourself.

When is Advent?

Advent begins four Sundays before December 25, sometimes in the last weekend of November, sometimes on the first Sunday in December and ends on Christmas Eve, thus there is some variation in its length.

Why light candles?

The light of the candles itself becomes an important symbol of the season. The light reminds us that:

 • Jesus is the Light of the world that permeates the darkness of our lives to bring newness, life, and hope.

 • We are called to be a light to the world as we reflect the light of God's grace to others (Isaiah 42:6).

Each week as we light the candles it symbolizes the various aspects of our waiting experience. The lighting of the candles over the four-week period, also illustrates the darkness of fear and hopelessness receding and the shadows of sin falling away as more and more light is shed into the world. With the lighting of each new candle, we are reminded that something is happening, and that more is yet to come. Finally, as the Christ candle is lit at Christmas, the light that has come into the world is plainly visible, and believers rejoice that God has done what He promised to do from the very beginning.

The first candle of Advent is the Prophet's candle or the Hope candle and it always focuses our hearts on the hope of the first Advent promised by the prophets. The second candle of Advent is the Bethlehem or the Peace candle.

The remaining three candles of Advent deal with the various parts of the Advent story. They may vary from church to church or even from year to year. The sequence for the remaining three Sundays might be Bethlehem, Shepherds and Angels (or Love, Joy and Peace). No matter what sequence is used, the Scripture reading, prayers, lighting of the candles, all center on unfolding the story of rescue and redemption through God's grace in the birth of Jesus.

I have chosen to go the route of Bethlehem, Shepherds and Angels.

FIRST SUNDAY OF ADVENT

*Our hope is based on knowing that God will do what He said He would do,
and so we wait expectantly knowing that Jesus is coming back!!!*

The Prophet's Candle - Hope

As we light the very first candle of the Advent season, our attention is centered
on the hope of the coming Messiah, the Anointed One. His coming is woven
like a golden thread all the way through Old Testament history. God's people
were stubborn and sinful, abused by power hungry kings, often led astray
by self-centered prophets and halfhearted religious leaders, which resulted
in many longing for God to raise up a new king who would lead them in
righteousness and truth. They longed for a return of God's dynamic presence in
their midst.

And so, God revealed to the true prophets that He would not leave His people
without a true Shepherd. The people waited, fully expecting a new earthly
king to come and set them free. However, their expectations fell far short of
God's revelation of Himself in Christ. So, when their king came, most of them
missed Him. The new king came, but His Kingdom was not of this world. God,
Himself, came in the form of a baby to set them free, and give them citizenship
in heaven.

And yet, the world is not yet fully redeemed. The pain, sin and brokenness of
this world leave us with expectation, with hope, waiting for God's new work
in history, the Second Advent (Second Coming of the Christ child), in which
He will again reveal Himself to the world. And because of their frailty and
ours we understand in a profound sense that on that day, once again, the best,
the highest of our expectations will fall far short of what our Lord's Second
Coming will reveal!

And so, we light the first candle of Hope.

Celebrating Advent is counter-cultural. Advent challenges us to wait, to hold off on celebrating Christmas until we've prepared ourselves. If we don't plan for Advent our lives will be shaped by the frenzy of the holiday season. Won't you take the time this season to prepare your heart for Christmas by reading the Scriptures below? Do not miss the reason for the season!

So my question is this, "Have you believed in Jesus as Savior and Lord? Are you ready for the Second Coming? What must you do to help others get ready for His coming?" Remember you are the light to a lost and dying world. May you give an account of the hope that is within you this Christmas season!

Bible reading for the first week of Advent:

Psalm 25:1-10
Jeremiah 33:14-16
Isaiah 11:1-10
Luke 1:26-38
Luke 21:25-36
Isaiah 7:10-14
Matthew 1:18-24
1 Thessalonians 3:9-13

Have you ever read something only to find that you don't remember what you have read? I have found that engaging with text in tangible ways helps embed what I've read in both my mind and my heart.

Because I know that not everyone has journaled in this way before, and I don't want you to miss anything, I've added journal prompts to help you out. They alert you to

   ᛗ Jesus' name and character traits
   + Actions to take
   (Not everything is marked)

At the end of each day I have included a journal page. Write down any insights you gained from reading the Scriptures given, answers to questions, names of people etc.

First Sunday Journal

DAILY DEVOTIONALS - WEEK ONE

Monday

⛫ Jesus is the Light of the world!

I am the Lord; I have called you in righteousness; I will take you by the hand and keep you; I will give you as a covenant for the people, a light for the nations. - Isaiah 42:6

The light of the candles itself becomes an important image of the season. The light reminds us that:
- Jesus is the light of the world that comes into the darkness of our lives to bring new life, and hope.
- We are called to be a light to the world reflecting the light of God's grace to others (Isaiah 42:6).

⛫ God the Creator of the heavens and the earth promised His Servant (Jesus) that He had been called to perform God's gospel plan for the world. Because the Lord would take hold of the Servant's hand, He would be empowered to carry out God's plan.

Because of His death and resurrection, the Servant was also assured He would fulfill God's covenant promises to Israel and also be a light of promise for the Gentiles. And that one day there will be a glorious kingdom, and God will bring justice to the nations. (Isaiah 42:1) "Jesus is the light of the world", (John 8:12) and that includes the Gentiles!

We too are called to share the gospel of Jesus Christ with the world. God has given us the Holy Spirit to empower us to share His gospel message with all He brings across our path. We are both called and empowered to share the gospel. Unless we obey by living out what we know is truth, we are not fulfilling our part of God's plan in His bigger story.

Something to think about

Christmas, with all the lights of the season shining all around us, is the perfect time to share with those who haven't yet heard. However, in order to have the most impact amidst the busyness of the season, it is important to prepare for and be alert to the opportunities all around you. It can be intimidating at first but be courageous, take the first step and God will pour out His grace enabling you to share. Each time you do, you will become more and more confident. In order to be prepared to reflect God's grace to others pray and ask God to:

- Open your eyes to opportunities to share the gospel with those around you. As God opens the door walk through it and share the gospel. (You may want to use the journal pages to write the stories of those experiences. For example, HOW God opened the door, WHERE He opened it, WHO it was opened for and HOW they responded.)
- Give you names of people to share the gospel with.
  (Write their names below)

Start a list of Jesus' names and character traits you learn each day on the **Jesus' Names and Character Traits** list in the back of the book.

Devotional Week One - Monday

DAILY DEVOTIONALS - WEEK ONE

Tuesday

Our hope is based on knowing God will do what He said He would do!

In those days Judah will be saved, and Jerusalem will dwell securely. And this is the name by which it will be called: 'The LORD is our righteousness.' For thus says the LORD: David shall never lack a man to sit on the throne of the house of Israel, and the Levitical priests shall never lack a man in my presence to offer burnt offerings, to burn grain offerings, and to make sacrifices forever. – Jeremiah 33:16-18

The days Jeremiah is talking about have yet to come, but a day is coming when Jesus will return and restore His people and their land. In that day their promised King will reign in righteousness and His name is "The Lord our Righteousness." God's promise to David that He would raise up a descendant to sit on the throne forever was fulfilled at the birth of Jesus; and God's promise to Phineas of a perpetual priesthood will be fulfilled when Jesus returns.

Our hope is based on knowing God will do what He said He would do! During the first week we light the first candle of Expectation or Hope. Not the hope that "wishes something will happen" but a Hope that knows it will happen.

Because God was right about the First Advent, in that it happened exactly as the prophets declared hundreds of years earlier, so it will be with the second. And so we wait expectantly knowing that Jesus is coming back!!!

Something to think about

Do you really believe Jesus is coming back? If so, are you living as though He may show up at any time? Explain your answer.

How should really believing Jesus is coming back impact the way you live your life?

Is there anything you would need to change about the way you are living? Take time to ask God to show you things that need to be changed, then make a plan to change. (Write them below).

Wednesday

What God requires Jesus provides.

In those days Judah will be saved, and Jerusalem will dwell securely. And this is the name by which it will be called: 'The LORD is our righteousness.' For thus says the LORD. David shall never lack a man to sit on the throne of the house of Israel, and the Levitical priests shall never lack a man in my presence to offer burnt offerings, to burn grain offerings, and to make sacrifices forever. – Jeremiah 23:5-6

King Zedekiah had imprisoned the prophet Jeremiah. Babylon's armies were advancing on Jerusalem. The streets of Jerusalem would soon be filled with the bodies of her own people. Jeremiah's prophecies of judgment were coming true. Yet, in the midst of adversity, Jeremiah spoke words of hope and of restoration.

It was in this dark hour of judgment and failure that God revealed to His people another of His names, Jehovah-Tsidkenu, the Lord our Righteousness. And with that revelation came a new covenant, the covenant of grace—and with it a new heart. The message of hope and restoration is that what God requires, Jesus provides!

Righteousness is more than goodness, it is a right standing with God. To be righteous is to do what God says is right, to live according to His standards. But righteousness in man requires a new heart. And God made a provision for a new heart!

I will put my law within them, and on their heart I will write it...for I will forgive their iniquity, and their sin I will remember no more.
(Jeremiah 31:33-34)

All this—a new covenant and a new heart—will come because of a Righteous Branch named Jehovah-Tsidkenu, the Lord our Righteousness. You can be right with God. You can be righteous. You do not have to live caught up in an endless cycle of sin and failure. This Righteous Branch is the fulfillment of God's promise to David. The Righteous Branch who will reign as king and do justice and righteousness is Jesus.

How can a man be made righteous? At Calvary's cross "He made Him who knew no sin to be sin on our behalf that we might become the righteousness of God" (2 Corinthians 5:21) – even "the righteousness of God through faith in Jesus Christ for all those who believe." (Romans 3:22)

We were created for works of righteousness. We are not righteous in and of ourselves, but Jehovah-Tsidnkenu in us is! Jesus will enable us to do what God has called us to do.

Daily Bible reading
Hebrews 8:6-13
Jeremiah 31:33-34
Jeremiah 23:5-6
2 Corinthians 5:20-21
Romans 3:21-26

Something to think about

Sometimes it can be hard to believe that God accepts us - that He's forgiven us. Some of us can really be hard on ourselves, and wonder if we really are saved, and right with God. Are you finding it hard to believe that you could ever find favor with God? This name brings comfort.

Are you in a crisis, wondering where God is and what He's doing? This name is a reassurance. Are you working hard at getting God to like you so that you can get into heaven? You can do your very best and be on your best behavior, but it will never come up to God's righteousness standard. Romans 3:23 tells us "There is none righteous, not even one." "All have sinned and fall short of the glory of God." The name reveals that we CAN'T do it without help! Jesus will enable you to do what God has called you to do!

When you became a believer you didn't automatically become righteous in all your thinking, speaking and living! Those who've been declared righteous in God's sight, He calls to be like Him. When you understand that the Lord became your righteousness, you are called to make consistent choices to offer yourself as an instrument of righteousness. (Romans 6:13) The Lord our Righteousness challenges us in our spiritual growth.

How does knowing and understanding the Lord our Righteousness bring you hope and restoration? (Write it out below)

🏰 Add new names for **God and His character traits** to your list.

DAILY DEVOTIONALS - WEEK ONE

Thursday

Jesus is God's plan for a promised deliverer! He is our rescuer!

She will bear a son, and you shall call his name Jesus, for he will save his people from their sins. – Matthew 1:21

Joseph had just found out that Mary, whom he was engaged to, was pregnant. In that culture to not be married and to be pregnant brought shame on not only the girl but also on the father of the baby and the family. Joseph didn't want to disgrace her and was secretly thinking about sending her away to have the baby when an angel appeared to him in a dream and explained Mary's pregnancy.

At the same time the angel told Joseph the baby would be a boy and to name him "Jesus," because he would save His people from their sins.

Actually, the baby boy was given two names - Jesus and Immanuel. Jesus, revealed His mission, to "save His people from their sins." Immanuel (which we'll look at tomorrow) revealed who He was in that redemptive mission, God is with us to save and also to judge.

Jesus means Savior, salvation is the purpose of His mission here on earth. His death and resurrection are the foundation of our salvation. As the Savior, Jesus is God's plan for a promised deliverer, who rescues man from sin and death into immortality and life. Jesus is the hope of the believer.

Jesus, there is no other name under heaven by which we must be saved.
– Acts 4:12

Matthew 1:18-25
Acts 13:23-25
Titus 2:11-14, 3:4-8
Philippians 3:20-21

Something to think about

God's plan from the very beginning was that Jesus would come to rescue His people from sin and death. Jesus' first coming, His death, burial and resurrection accomplished His purpose of coming. Because of salvation we have the power to overcome sin and have hope for the future. This is what separates us from the world.

The way others know we are God's people is by the way we live! We are to do life in such a way that there is no question in the minds of all who are watching that we are God's children. We can say we are a believer all day long but if we are not living in obedience to God's Word and instead live like everyone else in the world, we have no evidence that we are the children of God. From the beginning God made a distinction between light and darkness, His chosen people the Jews and the nations surrounding them and now believers and unbelievers. John tells us in 1 John 3:10 that the children of God and the children of the devil are obvious.

Does your walk and your talk match who you say you are? At home, in public and at church?

✝ Self Evaluation: When others look at your lifestyle, what do they see? List below what distinguishes you as a child of God other than your profession or church attendance.

If your friends, family, co-workers etc. were asked if you were a Christian what would they say? What is the evidence they would point to?

Is there anything in your life that may be clouding the vision of those who are watching? Take time today and ask God to show you anything that may be a distraction to them. If He does, write it down. Pray and confess it. Do whatever it takes to get rid of it!

Remember grace is greater than all of your sins!

Friday

God is with us!

Therefore the Lord Himself will give you a sign: Behold, a virgin will be with child and bear a son, and she will call His name Immanuel. - Isaiah 7:14

The essence of this passage and event in history is not merely that a baby was born, but that God became a baby. Not only did Jesus come to do the Father's will, but He came to put God on display to all who were watching, so that we would know what it is like to have God with us, as the name Immanuel, defines.

This powerful truth spoken 700 years before Jesus was even born is still relevant and much needed today!

Everywhere you turn people are in crisis. Many are in the hardest situations they have ever faced: cancer diagnosis, marriage problems, prodigal children, and great loss just to name a few! It is easy to get sucked into thinking that God has no idea what's going on, that He's lost control or that He has forgotten you!

His Word says He gives us a future and a hope. Life may be so overwhelming we may not be able to see it. We may not even be aware of His Presence on the most difficult days. But He hasn't abandoned us, and He never will.

In those times it is important to keep a vertical focus, remembering the gift of Jesus Christ, Immanuel, not just at Christmas, but also all year long! In both seasons of celebration and in seasons of brokenness, He's still with us. No matter what is going on around you don't lose focus! Even when it looks like God is nowhere around, He is with you! Realizing He is ever present in your life affords you the power to accomplish His plan and purposes for you.

We don't have to be afraid of the storms of life, uncertainty of the future, or changing times.

⌂ He is "God with us," our Refuge and Strength, our Savior and Lord.

Daily Bible reading
Isaiah 7:10-14

Something to think about

"Immanuel" describes who Jesus is – "God with us." If Jesus came to put God on display so that we would know what it is like to have God with us, and Jesus lives in us, how should we live in order that all who are watching would know God?

How does knowing and understanding God as Immanuel, bring hope when you are walking through difficult circumstances? How will that affect those who are watching?

⌂ Add Jesus' name and characteristics to your list. Don't forget the verses.

DAILY DEVOTIONALS - WEEK ONE

Saturday

Nothing is impossible for God!

May it be done according to Your Word. – Luke 1:38

Can you imagine Mary's surprise when she heard Gabriel's greeting? "Greetings you who are highly favored! The Lord is with you!" No wonder she was afraid and puzzled by the message delivered by the angel. After her heart stopped racing and she began to breathe again, her head must have been a swirl with questions. Why is an angel talking to me? In what way was she "highly favored" by God? How was God with her?

Mary's response reveals her humility and honesty before God. When she woke up that morning, she never expected to see an angel and receive special favors from heaven. She probably even wondered, why her, a poor girl from Nazareth? She was just an ordinary girl.

Gabriel then gave her the good news, she would become the mother of the promised Messiah and she was to name Him Jesus ("Jehovah is salvation") for He will save His people from their sins. In doing so, he confirmed both the deity and humanity of Jesus. As Mary's son He would be human; and as the Son of the Highest, He would be the Son of God, fulfilling the prophecy "For unto us a Child is born [His humanity], unto us a Son is given[His deity]." (Isaiah 9:6)

Mary asked Gabriel a very logical question, "How will this be, since I am a virgin?" (Luke 1:34)
This was not a question born from unbelief; rather it was a confession of faith. Mary knew what would happen, but she didn't know how it would happen. She believed the promise, but she just couldn't understand the execution of it. How

could a virgin have a baby? After all, this had never happened before and in her mind (and in the mind of men) it was impossible.

Gabriel ended his message by giving Mary a word of encouragement. Her aged relative Elizabeth was with child, proving that "with God nothing is impossible." And Mary's response, born out of belief, was to surrender herself to God as His willing servant. "Behold, I am the servant of the Lord; let it be to me according to your word." (Luke 1:30)

Mary experienced God's Grace, and believed His Word, and therefore she could be used by the Spirit to accomplish the will of God.

> ### *Daily Bible reading*
> Luke 1:26-38
> Isaiah 9:6-7

Something to think about

This was the second birth announcement Gabriel had delivered. The first one was delivered to Zacharias. Zacharias and Elizabeth were a faithful couple who both belonged to the priestly line. In the midst of a godless culture they were faithful to obey the Scripture and live blamelessly.

They had no children, which was a continual matter of prayer. Little did they know that God would answer their prayers in their old age and give them a son who would be the forerunner for the coming King!

Zacharias was frightened when Gabriel appeared by the altar, the angel told him not to fear. Imagine how excited Zacharias must have been when he heard they were going to have a son. However, undeterred by the fact that an angel showed up and announced God's Word, he took a horizontal look at himself and his wife, rather than a vertical look at God and decided that the birth of a son was impossible.

Despite being a priest and knowing what God's word said, Zacharias responded in unbelief. Zacharias was really questioning God's ability to do what He said He would do! As a result, Zacharias was struck mute until the Word was fulfilled!

God kept His promise, despite Zacharias' unbelief, and Elizabeth conceived a son in her old age.

Before we criticize Zacharias too much, we should examine ourselves and see how strong our own faith is. Do you really believe God will do what He said he would do? Don't say "yes" too quickly! It is not enough to simply say you believe. The way you prove to yourself and those around you is to believe and then rest in that belief.

+ Make a list of promises God has given you both in the Word and in your prayer time. Then write down how God answered those promises. How did you respond between the promise and the answer?

Do you think that your physical, emotional or educational limitations would keep God from doing what He said He would do? Ask God to search your heart and see if there is anything keeping you from totally surrendering yourself to God. If and when He does, don't discount it. Satan would love nothing more than to deceive you into thinking God is not greater than your limitations, keeping you ineffective in doing what He has called you to do.

When Mary said, "May it be done to me according to Your word," (Luke 1:38), it meant that from then on, her life would be a part of the fulfillment of divine prophecy.

Your life may not be part of the fulfillment of prophecy, however God does have a plan and purpose for your life, which includes good deeds, determined from the foundation of the world.

Have you totally surrendered your life (every aspect) to God in order for those plans to be fulfilled?

Mary's believing response was to surrender herself to God as His willing servant. She experienced the grace of God, believed the Word of God, and therefore she could be used by the Spirit to accomplish the will of God. How will you respond?

⌂ Add to your list of Jesus' names and characteristics.

Devotional Week One - Saturday

SECOND SUNDAY OF ADVENT

Bethlehem is a story about a humble couple on an unwanted journey, at an inconvenient time, to visit a tiny insignificant town.

The Bethlehem Candle - Peace

Today we light the second candle, the Bethlehem candle represents peace. It symbolizes the preparations being made to receive the Christ child. Bethlehem is a story about a humble couple on an unwanted journey, at an inconvenient time, to visit a tiny insignificant town.

Augustus Caesar was ruling in Rome and had issued an executive order that a census was to be taken. From the beginning God, in His sovereignty, had a plan. Caesar, unknowingly, played an important part in God's plan.

Mary and Joseph had to leave Nazareth so that they could register in Bethlehem, because Joseph was of the house and family of David. God used Caesar's directive to move Mary, pregnant and due at any time, along with Joseph, eighty miles from Nazareth to Bethlehem only to find that there was no room for them at the inn. So this humble couple embarked on this unwanted journey, at an inconvenient time not knowing that God had orchestrated these events so that the prophecy and the Scriptures would be fulfilled.

While some might have thought God was starting all over again, He was fulfilling what He had planned from the beginning. David's depraved line had been cut down like a dead tree but, as Isaiah expressed it, "a shoot [the Messiah] will come up from the stump of Jesse." (Isaiah 11:1) God had promised that the Savior would be a Jew, from the tribe of Judah and the family of David, born of a virgin in Bethlehem, the city of David, ruler in Israel, eternal and divine, a shepherd to His people. All of this occurred just as the Scriptures said.

This One will be our peace and deliverer! (Micah 5:5-6)

As we draw nearer to the birth of Jesus, we begin to see just how specific God was about giving His people "directions" to the main event! In Micah 5, we read a prophecy that occurred more than 700 years before the birth of Christ and yet it's as specific as if it were spoken right before! When the magi arrive at Herod's residence, they explain to the king that Jesus is supposed to be born in Bethlehem by quoting these very Scriptures. God did exactly what He said He would do!

Bethlehem was the smallest clan of Judah. It was a very insignificant town just outside of Jerusalem. Yet God did not choose Jerusalem for the birthplace of Messiah. God loved the world so much that He chose a tiny insignificant town as the location for the birth of the One who would literally change the world. This is the first of many reminders that God loves even the insignificant of the world, and in fact demonstrates this several times in the weeks to come leading up to the Messiah's birth.

One day there will be peace on earth and righteousness will reign. Jerusalem will become the capital of the world, and there will be no more war. How can this happen? Through the promise of Micah 5, the Deliverer will come. The Jewish leadership rejected their Prince of Peace, so there has been no peace in the world. But when Christ returns to earth, He will establish His kingdom of peace, just like God said He would, and there will be no more war!

Meanwhile, we can have peace in our hearts by trusting Christ as Savior. Jesus is calling. If you haven't already, will you make the decision to trust the Lord and obey Him today?

Bible reading for the first week of Advent:

Luke 2:1–7
Matthew 2:1–2, 9-11
Micah 5:2–6
Malachi 3:1–4
Luke 1:68–79
Mark 1:1-3
Matthew 3:1-6
Isaiah 9:6-7
Romans 5:1

Read the words to this familiar Christmas hymn.

O Little Town of Bethlehem

O little town of Bethlehem, how still we see thee lie!
Above thy deep and dreamless sleep the silent stars go by.
Yet in thy dark streets shineth the everlasting Light;
The hopes and fears of all the years are met in thee tonight.
For Christ is born of Mary, and gathered all above,
While mortals sleep, the angels keep their watch of wondering love.
O morning stars together, proclaim the holy birth,
And praises sing to God the King, and peace to men on earth!
How silently, how silently, the wondrous Gift is giv'n;
So God imparts to human hearts the blessings of His Heav'n.
No ear may hear His coming, but in this world of sin,
Where meek souls will receive Him still, the dear Christ enters in.
Where children pure and happy pray to the blessèd Child,
Where misery cries out to Thee, Son of the mother mild;
Where charity stands watching and faith holds wide the door,
The dark night wakes, the glory breaks, and Christmas comes once more.
O holy Child of Bethlehem, descend to us, we pray;
Cast out our sin, and enter in, be born in us today.
We hear the Christmas angels the great glad tidings tell;
O come to us, abide with us, our Lord Emmanuel!
Songwriters: Steven V. Taylor / Phillips Brooks / Lewis H. Redner
Public Domain

So my question is this, What about you? Do you want peace this Christmas? Jesus is our Peace! In the busyness of the season will you make room for Christ, or will you miss Him? One can't help but think of the innkeeper, would he have given up his room had he known who needed it?

If you have not done so already won't you ask the Christ child to enter in and be born in you today?

If He has already entered in, begin to prepare your heart to celebrate His birth in the upcoming weeks. You have "the One who is our Peace" dwelling within. – May you walk in His Peace this Christmas season.

Second Sunday Journal

DAILY DEVOTIONALS - WEEK TWO

Monday

Bethlehem - A tiny insignificant town.

But you, O Bethlehem Ephrathah, who are too little to be among the clans of Judah, from you shall come forth for Me One who is to be ruler in Israel, whose coming forth is from of old, from ancient days. (Micah 5:2)

Bethlehem was in the district of Ephrathah, (distinguishing it from Bethlehem to the north). It is a tiny insignificant town too small to have a place of importance among the families of Judah. Yet Bethlehem was destined to be exalted throughout the world, for the Messiah was to be born in this humble place. Christ's birth would bring honor to the place of His birth, and He would not receive honor because of where He was born. Even today many visit Bethlehem because it is the birthplace of Jesus the Christ, not because it is a large prestigious city.

However, though the town was insignificant in itself, this was not a barrier to God. Out of it He would bring the future ruler of Israel, just as He had once brought David! Bethlehem also represents God's promise of a Davidic descendant whose throne and kingdom would be eternal and who would mediate God's blessings to all mankind. This was all according to His plan from the very beginning.

Daily Bible reading
Micah 5:2-5
1 Samuel 17:12
Luke 2:4, 11

Something to think about

It is a biblical principle, that exaltation by God must always be launched from humility. (1 Corinthians 1:18-31, Philippians 2:5-11)

Do you ever feel invisible? Worthless? Insignificant? Do you wonder what you have to offer God? Be encouraged, throughout history God has chosen the humble, those without means, status or platforms to be exalted to His platform from which to make God known to all who see. He most often uses the ordinary to do the extraordinary!

Do you have a hard time trusting God in your circumstances? Are you in a difficult season of life and you wonder if God's promises are true today? Once again, we see God fulfilling His promise of long ago. He has a long track record of doing what He said He would do! It may not be on our timetable, but you can trust Him even in the darkest of times!

+ Today take time to list what you believe you need from God. Then use a concordance or Google to find verses that speak to that need and write them on the journal page below so you can refer back to them to remind you when life gets hard.

For example: Are you feeling abandoned? "For the LORD your God is the one who will go with you; He will not leave you or abandon you." (Deuteronomy 31:6) Write this verse on the journal page and watch for God's hand at work and how He teaches you to know the truth of this verse. Then write it down as a tangible reminder to you each time you feel abandoned!

Devotional Week Two - Monday

DAILY DEVOTIONALS - WEEK TWO

Tuesday

Wise men still seek Him

Where is He who has been born King of the Jews? - Matthew 2:2

Sometime after Jesus was born in Bethlehem, (in the days of Herod) wise men (magi) from the east, (Babylon) arrived in Jerusalem. Magi are a caste of wise men specializing in astronomy, astrology and natural sciences. They were wealthy, and they were scholars--scientists in their own right. God had given them a special sign, a miraculous star that announced the birth of the King. They were not surprised. They had been expecting it. You might be asking "How did they know to expect it if they lived so far away?" Daniel, when he was taken captive by King Nebuchadnezzar, became one of the magi, or Chaldeans as they were sometimes known. Daniel's writings were kept by the Jewish people since they recognized him as a prophet. However, the magi, or Chaldeans, also studied his writings because they recognized him as one of their own.

The star led them to Jerusalem and upon their arrival they asked, "Where is He who is born King of the Jews? For we saw His star in the east and have come to worship Him." Upon hearing this Herod was troubled and all Jerusalem (the religious leaders) were too.

God's prophets had told them that the King would be born in Bethlehem. Herod relayed the birthplace to them and sent them to Bethlehem. After hearing from the king, they left, and the star, which they had seen in the east, led them to the place where the Child was. There they worshiped the Christ Child and gave Him their gifts of gold, frankincense and myrrh.

We don't know how many Wise Men were actually there, although from the three gifts given, some have assumed there were three, but we don't know for sure. It is interesting that these men who came seeking the King were Gentiles.

Once again a prophecy was fulfilled! So far we have seen the following prophecies fulfilled: How He was to be born (Isaiah 7:14, Matthew 1:18-20), where He would be born (Micah 5:2, Luke 2:1-7) and now that He was the King! (Matthew 2:5)

Daily Bible reading
Matthew 2:1-16
Isaiah 7:14
Matthew 1:18-20
Micah 5:2
Luke 2:1-7
Matthew 3:5

Something to think about

The Wise Men waited expectantly for the birth of the King, and when they saw the star announcing His birth they, travelled for months seeking the Christ Child. Herod was afraid of the King, who brought a threat to his throne, and wanted to destroy Him. The Jewish priests also knew that Messiah was coming, but they were ignoring the King. They knew the Scriptures and pointed others to the Christ Child but would not go worship Him themselves! Both Herod and the priests were five miles from the Son of God, yet they did not go see Him!

When the Wise Men, who were Gentiles, saw that star in the east, they set out with every intention of finding the newborn King. When the star stood over where the Child was, they were overwhelmed with great joy and they fell to the ground and worshiped Him! Then, opening their treasures, they presented Him with gifts of gold, frankincense and myrrh.

What about you? Are you intentionally seeking Him in every area of your life and overwhelmed with joy and delighting in Him when you do? Or are you more like Herod, afraid that he would be removed from his throne, no longer to rule? Perhaps you are more like the Pharisees, knowing what the Scriptures say and telling others about them, but ignoring them in your personal life?

Remember, wise men will seek Him!

Once again, God told men ahead of time what He was going to do and He did it! It did not always happen immediately, but it always happened in His time.

Are you standing at the crossroads of belief and unbelief? Be intentional. Repent. Make a conscious decision to step toward God, to lean into hope, to heed the call of heaven, to be all in. Press into the promises of God.

Write down your take away from today's reading.

DAILY DEVOTIONALS - WEEK TWO

Wednesday

⛶ The One who is our peace.

For to us a child is born, to us a son is given, and the government will be on his shoulders. And he will be called Wonderful Counselor, Mighty God, Everlasting Father, Prince of Peace. – Isaiah 9:6

In a broken world filled with war and violence, natural disasters, poverty, divided leadership, broken families… it's difficult to see how Jesus could be the all-powerful God who acts in human history and the personification of peace. But physical safety and political harmony don't necessarily reflect the kind of peace He's talking about.

⛶ God had promised a Redeemer. The Redeemer would come and bring to the world the dawning of a new day. But the prophet looked beyond the first advent of Christ to His second advent and the establishing of His righteous kingdom. Isaiah 9:6 proclaims both the humanity ("A Child is born") and the deity ("A Son is given") of the Lord Jesus Christ.

⛶ This Redeemer, the Messiah, is also called the Prince of Peace, the One who is our peace. We, who were once His enemies, can now have peace with God. The Prince of Peace not only is our peace that guards our hearts and our minds, but also He will keep those who trust Him and keep their thoughts focused on Him in perfect peace! (Isaiah 26:3) We have all of this because of Messiah's first coming.

⛶ But there's more. Isaiah not only prophesied the Messiah's first coming, He also prophesied Jesus' second coming and His ultimate Kingdom of righteousness. The Messiah will establish His kingdom of righteousness, justice and peace and rule forever just like God promised! This world and all its brokenness will be restored to what God had intended when He created it! No more war and violence, broken relationships, or heinous crimes against humanity.

Daily Bible reading
John 14:27
Isaiah 9:1-7
Luke 1:78-79
Luke 1:32-33
2 Samuel 7:16

Something to think about

Before becoming believers we were enemies with God. Because of Christ's sacrifice, we are restored to a relationship of peace with God. (Romans 5:1) This is the deep, abiding peace between our hearts and our Creator that cannot be taken away (John 16:7) and the ultimate fulfillment of Christ's work as Prince of Peace. We are to be reflections of God's love, joy and peace, which are indicators that the Holy Spirit is working in our lives.

Take time today to ask yourself if you are at peace with God? If the answer is no, pray asking God what is robbing you of your peace. When He shows you don't question it and don't say, "that isn't a problem." The enemy of your soul doesn't want you to be at peace with God and will lie to you to keep you at odds with the Father. Agree with God by confessing it as sin. Replace the lie you have believed with the Truth from God's word and then walk as though you believe it. Then thank God for the peace that passes understanding, which guides you into all righteousness.

You may want to write it down to read back over from time to time to help you become aware of those things have the potential to rob you of peace.

Have you ever said, "I just don't have peace about …" often that can be the Holy Spirit's leading to keep you from doing something God had not intended for you to do, even if it's a good thing. That lack of peace just might be what God uses to keep you walking on the path of His will. Write down when this happened and the result. In hindsight did you see what God was up to? What did you learn through that experience? Next time you don't have peace about something you are about to do, remember the Prince of Peace who resides in you may be using that as a warning that you are about to step into a danger zone. Don't ignore it!

Are there difficult people in your life who you find hard to love? God has called us to be diligent to preserve the unity of the Spirit in the bond of peace. Jesus never promised easy, He only promised help. In fact, He told us to expect trouble and trials. But He also said that if we asked, He would give us peace that is beyond our understanding. No matter how hard our relationships are, we can ask for a peace that flows from God's love for us and doesn't depend on our own strength or our circumstances. Next time you find yourself faced with a difficult person stop, take a breath, pray and ask for help.

Add new name and characteristics for Jesus to your list.

Devotional Week Two - Wednesday

DAILY DEVOTIONALS - WEEK TWO

Thursday

His people are blessed with Peace.

The LORD gives His people strength; the LORD blesses His people with peace.
Psalm 29:11

We are living in a broken world filled with darkness, hatred and deceit, deserving of judgment. All over the world believers are being persecuted, even killed for their faith. Yet we are called to live here in peace and be a light in the darkness. How is that possible? Only by being totally surrendered to the One who is our peace, living in His strength, under His blessing of peace.
Peace is a priceless blessing God has designed specifically for His people as they walk righteously in a world gone dark. It's an endless peace, not just for today, but also through eternity. When the thunder of God's wrath makes those who are not His tremble, His children will lift their heads with joy. Even if darkness surrounds them, they can stand strong with an inner peace knowing that they will not be overcome!

What about you? Are you fearful as you watch what is going on around you in these days of uncertainty? Refocus. Rehearse what you know to be true. Rest knowing that God will do what He said He would do.

Daily Bible reading
Psalm 29
Mark 4:36-41
Matthew 8:1-16

Something to think about

Read through Psalm 29. Did you notice anything that is repeated?

Now let's slow down and look at this Psalm one section at a time.

So you don't miss it, God's glory refers primarily to His majestic beauty and splendor and the recognition of it by mankind, and embraces His holiness.

Record the answers to the questions on the journal page.
Read verses 1-2. In these first two verses the sons of the mighty are told to "Ascribe to the Lord", in other words they are told to "give honor that is due His name." What is it that brings the Lord honor?

When that understanding of the Lord is grasped according to verse 2, what will be the result?

Read back through verses 3-9 underlining every mention of "The voice of the Lord" in your Bible. Did you notice how loud these verses sound? Make a list of all you learn about the voice of the Lord in these verses.

Did you notice that God created all of the things on your list? What does that say about His authority? Explain your answer.

In your own words write out what you learn about the voice of the Lord and how knowing those things have impacted you.

Verses 10-11 are the final verses and summary statement of this Psalm. Write down what you learn about the Lord in verse 10 and what He gives to His people in verse 11.

The God who created everything governed at the flood and forever by His power! And the One who is peace gives His people strength and blesses them with peace throughout eternity.

God's voice plays an important role in the Bible as a whole. The very first time we hear God's voice is at Creation when He said, "Let there be light!" God has been speaking light into the darkness ever since. Jesus rebuked the wind and said to the sea "Hush, be still." And the wind died down and it became perfectly calm. Jesus spoke, healing all who were ill (lepers, a centurion's servant and Peter's mother in law, and demons were cast out).

If all of that doesn't stir you to wonder, think about this, God's voice swaddled in the voice of a baby, who cannot yet speak, nursing at His mother's breast. That will move you to worship!

Devotional Week Two - Thursday

DAILY DEVOTIONALS - WEEK TWO

Friday

Are you looking for peace?

In Me you may have peace. In the world you will have tribulation. But take heart; I have overcome the world. – John 16:33

Jesus had just finished His last message to the disciples during their final meal together. They had just confessed their belief that He came from God. He took this opportunity to prepare them because He knew the tribulation they would soon face. In a world filled with hatred, war and uncertainty you can find peace only if you have first made peace with God.

It has been said that peace is defined as "the possession of adequate resources." As a believer in Jesus Christ, we have all the resources we need. Did you see the contrast in John16:33? Don't miss it! In Christ there is peace; in the world there is tribulation. We need to embrace our position in Christ, in doing so, it's the only way we can overcome the world and all of its hatred.

"In Me" is the key. In ourselves, we have nothing; but in Christ we have all we need. We have peace!

Every believer is either an overcomer or overcome. The world wants to overcome us, this is why Satan uses the world to persecute and pressure believers. The world wants us to conform and does not want us to be different. When we surrender to Christ and trust Him, He enables us to be overcomers. We are overcomers because He first overcame us!

Jesus has shown us how to overcome the world. He Himself was facing the hatred of the world and the devil, yet He would be able to endure the suffering and defeat the enemy. Our world is full of violence, and our daily lives can be marred by conflict and turmoil. But God promises His people a peace that surpasses all understanding.

When a man's ways please the LORD, He makes even his
enemies to be at peace with him. - Proverbs 16:7

Daily Bible reading
John 16:32-33
Proverbs 16:6-7

Something to think about

During the First World War, unofficial ceasefires took place along the Western Front. The week before Christmas both German and British soldiers exchanged Christmas greetings and sang songs between their trenches. It has been said that Silent Night was one of those songs sung at that time. Occasionally the tension lessened to the point that the soldiers would walk across to their "enemies" bearing gifts.

This truce is often seen as a symbolic moment of peace in the middle of one of the most violent events in modern history.

Read the words to this song letting them sink into your soul. Now softly sing the song.

Silent Night
Silent night, holy night!
All is calm, all is bright
Round yon Virgin Mother and Child!
Holy Infant so tender and mild,
Sleep in heavenly peace! (2x)

Silent night, holy night!
Shepherds quake at the sight!
Glories stream from heaven afar,
Heavenly hosts sing Alleluia!
Christ, the Saviour is born!
Christ, the Saviour is born!

Silent night, holy night!
Son of God, love's pure light
Radiant beams from Thy holy face
With the dawn of redeeming grace,
Jesus, Lord, at Thy birth!
Jesus, Lord, at Thy birth!

Composed in 1818 by Franz Xaver Gruber to lyrics by Joseph Mohr
in the small town of Oberndorf bei Salzburg, Austria. Public Domain

That tiny baby, sleeping peacefully in the manger is our Peace! His birth
brought an everlasting peace to all who will invite Him in. What about you?
Have you invited Him in? If not, you can do so today.

DAILY DEVOTIONALS - WEEK TWO

Saturday

On Christmas Eve in 1865, Phillips Brooks, a young American Episcopalian, rode on horse back from Jerusalem to Bethlehem, to assist at the midnight service in the Church of the Nativity. Two years later he was inspired by the experience to write this carol for the children in his Sunday school.

Today, as the second week of Advent comes to an end, read through the words of this children's song turned Christmas carol.

O little town of Bethlehem
O little town of Bethlehem
How still we see thee lie!
Above thy deep and dreamless sleep
The silent stars go by.
Yet in thy dark streets shineth
The everlasting Light,
The hopes and fears of all the years
Are met in thee tonight.

For Christ is born of Mary
And, gathered all above,
While mortals sleep, the angels keep
Their watch of wondering love.
O morning stars, together
Proclaim the holy birth,
And praises sing to God the King,
And peace to men on earth.

How silently, how silently,
the wondrous gift is given.
So God imparts to human hearts

the blessings of His heaven.
No ear may hear His coming,
but in this world of sin,
where meek souls will receive him,
still the dear Christ enters in.

O holy Child of Bethlehem,
Descend to us, we pray,
Cast out our sin, and enter in,
Be born in us today.
We hear the Christmas angels
The great glad tidings tell,
O come to us, abide with us,
Our Lord Emmanuel!
Songwriters: Phillips Brooks, Lewis Redner, Public Domain

Within the beauty of "O Little Town of Bethlehem" is one of God's promises from the prophet Micah.

But you, O Bethlehem Ephrathah, who are too little to be among the clans of Judah, from you shall come forth for me one who is to be ruler in Israel, whose coming forth is from of old, from ancient days. (Micah 5:2)

The last verse is a prayer. In fact, it is such an awesome Christmas prayer that we sing it with evangelistic passion.

THIRD SUNDAY OF ADVENT

The Shepherd's Candle - Joy

It is the third Sunday of Advent, and today we light the Shepherd's Candle. The lighting of this candle is a reminder that God came for the most unlikely, insignificant people, the outcasts, the un-good. By that I mean this, the first announcement of the Messiah's birth was given to a group of shepherds! (Luke 2:8-14) There was not a more unlikely group to receive such an important announcement, unless maybe it was the Gentiles.

Think about it. If you were making the announcements, who would you pick to hear it first? The high priest? The whole company of priests? The religious ruling body called the Sanhedrin? King Herod? All of these would be possibilities. But God chose none of them.

The People Who Heard

God sent the angels to announce the birth not to the important and the elite, but to the un-good, the outcasts.

Shepherding sheep in Jesus' day was not the honorable profession it had been in the days of King David. In the New Testament period shepherds were considered ritually unclean because of their jobs, which meant they were excluded from temple worship. They had a reputation for being unreliable, dishonest, and were not even allowed to testify in court proceedings. It is even reported that one rabbi said, "Give no help to heathens or shepherds." In many ways they were the outcasts of that society. Shepherds were the lowest of the low.

God didn't seek out the religious leaders of the day, He came to the un-good, the outcasts! The message came to the shepherds because Christ came for everybody. All of this is a reminder that many times God does not call the rich and mighty but the poor and lowly.

For consider your calling, brethren, that there were not many wise according to the flesh, not many mighty, not many noble; but God has chosen the foolish things of the world to shame the wise, and God has chosen the weak things of the world to shame the things which are strong - 1 Corinthians 1:26-27

Can you imagine this group of shepherds out in the field when an angel suddenly appears? It was probably a very ordinary night. You have the feeling reading Luke's account that it was a quiet evening. And then SUDDENLY the sky exploded with light, the glory of God surrounded them and an angel appeared saying, "Fear not." Really? Don't be afraid? The message came to them right where they were, they didn't have to go anywhere to hear it. God sought them out in the fields and they were invited into God's glory and presence.

M Christ stepped out of heaven to be with us. He is Emmanuel. God seeks you out and pursues you wherever you may be!

They probably ignored the "Fear not" part of the greeting. It is hard to imagine that the shepherds suddenly quit shaking after the angel shared those words of comfort.

Then the angel says, "Behold!" (Luke 2:10) In Scripture this word almost always means something unusual, something completely unexpected is about to happen.

M The angel told the shepherds a baby was born in Bethlehem. This baby was the long-awaited Messiah. The angel described the child as the Savior for all people, Christ the Lord. (Luke 2:11)
By appearing to the shepherds, the angel revealed the grace of God to all mankind.

Behold, the announcement of the arrival of the Messiah has come to the shepherds, the un-good of Israel. A baby was born in Bethlehem, for them!

As if to punctuate the moment, a choir of angels appeared and sang a chorus:

Glory to God in the highest, and on earth peace among men with whom He is pleased. Glory to God in the highest BECAUSE the glory of God has visited the lowest! – (Luke 2:14)

The Place They Were Told

It shouldn't have been such a surprise. Everyone knew the Messiah would be born in Bethlehem, they just were not paying attention. The old rabbis taught that the announcement of His birth would be at Migdal Edar, or the "tower of the flock."

As for you, tower of the flock, Hill of the daughter of Zion, to you it will come— Even the former dominion will come, the kingdom of the daughter of Jerusalem. – Micah 4:8

Small rock towers were common in Judah. The shepherds used them as watch towers so they could see the surrounding area. They were so common that one might have asked, "Which tower?" The one outside Bethlehem of course!

Joy

The Shepherd's candle also symbolizes the Joy at the coming of Jesus. The first two Sundays of Advent focus on Preparation and Hope, this third Sunday shifts to an atmosphere of joy, anticipation and expectancy. The message to the shepherds was one of "good tidings of great joy."

What was the message? The good news of the gospel and that it is for everyone! (Luke 2:10)
- Jesus came to be your Savior. (Luke 2:11)
  He will save His people from their sins. (Matthew 1:21)
- Jesus came to be your Lord, your master. (Luke 2:11)
  If you confess with your mouth, "Jesus is Lord" and believe in your heart that God raised Him from the dead, you will be saved. (Romans 10:9)

How did the Shepherds respond to this good news? They left everything and went immediately to Bethlehem to seek for themselves this baby wrapped in cloth lying in a manger, that the angel of the Lord had told them about.

After seeing Mary, Joseph and the baby who was lying in the manger, they shared the message of the gospel with everyone they saw. All who heard it were amazed at what the shepherds told them!

The shepherds, the un-good, the outcasts, were not only the first to hear the good news, they were also the first evangelists! You have to wonder if God had told the rich, the popular, and the religious leaders first, would they have responded in the same way?

The Shepherd's candle serves as a reminder that the Christmas message is one of rejoicing.

Daily Bible reading

Luke 1:46-55
Luke 2:8-20
Luke 3:7-18
Isaiah 35:1-10
Isaiah 12:2-6
Zephaniah 3:14, 20
Psalm 146-5-10
Matthew 11:2-11
Philippians 4:4-7
James 5:7-10

Something to think about

God uses people from all walks of life to spread the good news of His Son. God chose to use the shepherds to describe the vastness of His love for us. This week as we think about Advent, we discover that God does extraordinary things through ordinary people. God chose the insignificant of the day to reveal His magnificence.

God reminds us, "as you have done it to the least of these, you have done it to me!" (Matthew 25:45)

Read the words to this familiar song.

Read the words to this familiar song.

Joy to the World

Joy to the world, the Lord is come!
Let earth receive her King;
Let every heart prepare Him room,
And Heaven and nature sing,
And Heaven and nature sing,
And Heaven, and Heaven, and nature sing.

Joy to the earth, the Savior reigns!
Let men their songs employ;
While fields and floods, rocks, hills and plains
Repeat the sounding joy,
Repeat the sounding joy,
Repeat, repeat, the sounding joy.

No more let sins and sorrows grow,
Nor thorns infest the ground;
He comes to make His blessings flow
Far as the curse is found,
Far as the curse is found,
Far as, far as, the curse is found.

He rules the world with truth and grace,
And makes the nations prove
The glories of His righteousness,
And wonders of His love,
And wonders of His love,
And wonders, wonders, of His love.

Isaac Watts, based on Psalm 98, 96:11-12 and Genesis 3:17-18.
Public Domain

In even the darkest corners of the globe, Christ sets the captive free and puts a song in lonely hearts. He reigns as king in the lives of men. And He can bring joy to you if you really believe the message, "Joy to the world, the Lord is come."

This belief is not simply a mental assent. This belief instructs the mind, engages the heart and influences the will. In other words, you don't simply hear the message and walk away. It's a message you hear and become so passionate about that you can't stop thinking and talking about it. When you really believe Christ sets you free, it fills you with insurmountable joy.

You have heard the message, but do you really believe it?

When they saw the star, they rejoiced with exceeding great joy.
- Matthew 2:10

DAILY DEVOTIONALS - WEEK THREE

Monday

Jesus' birth drew the angels from heaven.

How amazed the angels must have been to see the Creator born as a creature, the Word coming as a tiny baby!

One night, outside the town of Bethlehem, shepherds were in the fields watching over their sheep. Suddenly, as if a star had burst, the glory of the Lord overpowered the night for the first time in centuries, and an honored angel of the Lord stepped forward, as the shepherds, terrified, likely recoiled in great fear despite his reassuring words.

"I announce to you good news, a great joy which shall be to all the people," the angel said. The Good News preached here is for everybody, not just the Jews. What was this good news? The gospel! God had sent a Savior to meet man's greatest need. It was a message of peace, which was much more than a truce in the battles of life. It brought peace with God, which brings well-being, that has more to do with character, than circumstances. The Law and even Jewish religion could not meet the needs of men's hearts. Then, God sent His Son! The long-expected Savior!

Job tells us that at the creation of the world, "the morning stars [angels] sang together and all the angels shouted for joy." (Job 38:7) Now the angels again joined voices at the beginning of the greatest creation of all—the birth of the Messiah, the firstborn of a new creation! The angels praised God at Creation, and now they praised Him at the beginning of the new creation. Angels glorify God as they witness God's plan unfold!

The whole purpose of the plan of salvation is to bring "glory to God." God's glory had dwelt in the tabernacle and in the temple, but had departed because of the nation's sin. Now God's glory was returning to earth in the person of His Son.

Then the angel gave the shepherds a sign to establish their faith. "You will find a baby wrapped in swaddling cloths and lying in a manger." (Luke 2:12) Perhaps other babies were born that night in the village of Bethlehem. But it was highly unlikely that the shepherds would find another newborn baby lying in a manger. This was not where they expected to find the future King!

Immediately after the message was given, as if that in itself was not stunning enough, it was punctuated by a choir made up of a multitude (more than one can count) Perhaps all of God's angels were present at this most amazing event ever! This choir of angels sang,

Glory to God in the highest, and on earth peace among those
with whom he is pleased! – Luke 2:14

Daily Bible reading
Luke 2:8-14

Something to think about

Read Luke 2:8-14.
- As you read, underline shepherds and draw a circle around angels.
- Make a list about everything you learned about the shepherds i.e., What were they doing? What was the message to them? What were they given? Etc.
- Make a list about everything you learn about the angels.
- After you have done this write down anything that stood out to you that you have not seen before, or that the Lord was speaking to you personally. Then determine what action you will take if you need to.

When Christ was here on earth, what set Him apart was that He distinguished Himself, and made Himself extraordinary, by His humility. Christ's life was punctuated with humility from His birth until His death on the cross. Can the same be said of you? Ask the Lord to show you if you are distinguishing yourself with instances of humility or by pride. If the answer is by pride, ask Him to show any area of your life you need to work on such as your academic, financial, or spiritual achievements? Perhaps in your relationships, marriage, or parenting? Don't answer too quickly, sit at His feet and wait for Him to answer. The enemy would love for you to be blinded from the truth!

✴ Notice the words of the angels' praise song. It began with a vertical focus as they glorified God in "the highest" heavens, and then focused horizontally as they sang, "on earth peace among those with whom He is pleased." What would your praise song sound like? Try writing your personal praise song to the Lord based on the example of the angels, in the journal pages.

Though the choir in Heaven played a major role, we on earth have the best part because we are the ones who receive God's grace. God became a man, not an angel. God redeemed us, not angels. Ours is the best part, and we will praise God for it for all eternity. Let that sink in!

Has God worked in your heart? Are you the object of His good pleasure? Then you have a song to sing, for the best part is yours!

Tuesday

Lovely simplicity of devotion and faith!

Yesterday we read about how an ordinary night watching their sheep, suddenly exploded into an extraordinary night filled with the glory of God, an angel giving a gospel presentation and a sign validating it to shepherds in the fields outside of Bethlehem! The message was punctuated by the voices of a multitude of angels surrounding them and praising God.

Once the messenger left, God's glory had faded, the music slipped away and the choir of angels returned to heaven. How did the shepherds respond? They responded with a lovely simplicity of devotion and faith!

Instead of being enamored with the performance, they were captivated by the message! They knew they had heard from the Lord, and without so much as a quarrel they made the decision to leave immediately in search of the sign given to them, a Baby wrapped in swaddling cloths lying in a manger, validating the humble spirit of these men.

The shepherds hurried to Bethlehem and found Mary, Joseph and the Baby lying in the manger, just as the angel had said. As they looked into the face of the Baby they saw God's plan for salvation. Having seen this they shared with the young parents the whole story about what the angel had said about the child and all that the multitude of angels had sung about His birth!

Seeing the baby Jesus was not enough for the shepherds. They had to share the story. Everyone they met heard from them about angelic visits, angelic songs of praise, and a trip to a manger to find the Baby of God's glory. Most important, they shared what had been told them about this child, the message of the gospel! All who heard stood in amazement and wonder at every word they had heard from the shepherds.

When was the last time you were struck by the wonder of the birth of Christ?

While the rest were struck by wonder, for Mary it went much deeper. She had incubated amazement for nine months, having heard Gabriel's announcement. Now she incubated experiences in her mind and dots were beginning to connect. Experiences that gradually became treasured memories, each showing something new and different about her Son, each confirming Gabriel's promise of greatness for this Son of David and Son of the Most High. Surely nothing was impossible with God.

We catch a glimpse of the depth of Mary's character; it was calm and deep, spiritually receptive and strong, steady and persevering in grace.

The shepherds came. They found in a manger what God told them to expect, the Savior, the Messiah, the Lord Himself. They told everyone they saw the good news! They went back to their flocks with deep, new emotions and a song of praise in their hearts, forever changed. They returned to the sheep never to be heard from again, but not forgotten! God did what He said He would do!

These shepherds, outcasts of society, were the first evangelists!

The child's birth was the realization of truth spoken by the prophets over the ages. Salvation was the purpose for which He was born. It was all part of God's plan from the beginning.

Daily Bible reading
Luke 2:15-20
Luke 1:30-38

Something to think about

+ Read today's devotional again writing down the answers to the following:
  - What did you learn about the shepherds?
  - What did they find when they arrived in Bethlehem?
  - How did they respond to what they saw?
  - Was seeing the baby enough for the shepherds? Explain your answer.
  - What did they share and to whom did they share it?
  - How did those listening respond to what they heard?
  - How was Mary's response different from the others? Explain your answer.
  - From all you read what made this baby different from every other baby that has been born?

The shepherds are good examples for us to imitate today. They received by faith the message God sent them and then responded with immediate obedience. Instead of being enamored by the performance, they were captivated by the message! After finding the Baby, they shared the good news with everyone they saw, "glorifying and praising God." They took the place of the angels! (Luke 2:13–14) Then they humbly returned to their duties, forever changed, they were new men going back to the same old job.

+ Answer the following questions

  - How do you respond to the Word of God? Do you read it and obey it immediately? Or do you read it checking it off your list of things to do but continue living your life as you always have?
  - When you attend church each week are you more enamored by the music and all that is going on? Or are you captivated by the message being proclaimed? What are you doing with what you have heard?
  - Perhaps you have heard and read the stories so many times that you have lost the wonder and amazement that the shepherds had. If so, ask God to restore to you the wonder of the most amazing story on earth. When He does, you too will not be able to stop telling others the message of the birth of the Baby, not just at Christmas but all throughout the year!
  - When was the last time you shared the gospel with those who have not yet heard?

+ Make a list of all those in your sphere of influence. Begin to pray for them asking God to open the door for you to share the gospel with them.

DAILY DEVOTIONALS - WEEK THREE

Wednesday

The first public announcement of Christ's birth.

The *First Noel*, a Christmas reminder that Christ came to rescue and redeem the whole world.

Have you ever really paid attention to the Christmas hymns we sing? I know that personally I love singing them. The message they bring builds a strong foundation on which to celebrate this season. It wasn't until recent years I began to pay attention to them and the message they deliver. I began to write the lyrics out and read through them slowly allowing the message to soak deep down into my soul like a healing salve.

Noel is a French word that means "birthday." The First Noel tells the story of the birth of Christ. The first public birth announcement was given to shepherds who were in the fields watching over their flocks.

In order for the whole story to be told, all six verses must be sung. It is interesting that the "King of Israel" was first announced to "certain poor shepherds" only, but the final verse says "let us all" and "mankind hath brought." It reminds us that God's plan was that Christ came to rescue and redeem the whole world.

Something to think about

† Read slowly through the hymn below and write out
- Who delivered the message?
- What is the message repeated in each verse?
- Who are the people that received it and what did you learn about each group?
- What sign were they given to find this baby?
- What will this King do?
- Who, according to the last verse, was also included in this wonderful message?

The First Noel
The First Noel, the Angels did say,
Was to certain poor shepherds in fields as they lay,
In fields where they lay keeping their sheep,
On a cold winter's night that was so deep.
Noel, Noel, Noel, Noel,
Born is the King of Israel!

They looked up and saw a star
Shining in the East beyond them far,
And to the earth it gave great light,
And so it continued both day and night.
Noel, Noel, Noel, Noel,
Born is the King of Israel!

And by the light of that same star
Three Wise men came from country far,
To seek for a King was their intent,
And to follow the star wherever it went.
Noel, Noel, Noel, Noel,
Born is the King of Israel!

This star drew nigh to the northwest,
O'er Bethlehem it took its rest,
And there it did both pause and stay,
Right o'er the place where Jesus lay.
Noel, Noel, Noel, Noel,
Born is the King of Israel!

Then entered in those Wise men three,
Fall reverently upon their knee,
And offered there in His presence
Their gold, and myrrh, and frankincense.
Noel, Noel, Noel, Noel,
Born is the King of Israel!

Then let us all with one accord
Sing praises to our heavenly Lord,
That hath made Heaven and earth of naught
And with his blood mankind has bought.
Noel, Noel, Noel, Noel,
Born is the King of Israel! Anonymous/Unknown before 1833.
Public Domain

The last verse of the song serves as a Christmas reminder that Christ came to redeem the whole world. Think about that for a minute, let it soak deep down into your soul. How will this reminder impact your life?

Now that you have taken a look at the lyrics to this song, how can you use this as a platform to share the message with those who have never heard it?

This Christmas as you sing this song, pray for all who are listening to hear the song's message and that it would take root in their hearts.

DAILY DEVOTIONALS - WEEK THREE

Thursday

What a glorious day!

The Shepherd's candle also symbolizes the joy at the coming of Jesus. The first two Sundays of Advent focus on Preparation and Hope, this third Sunday shifts to an atmosphere of joy, anticipation and expectancy. The message to the shepherds was one of "good tidings of great joy." It serves as a reminder that the Christmas message is one of rejoicing.

Joy to the Word, written by Isaac Watts, was not written to be a Christmas song. Originally this song was written about the second coming of the Lord.

As you hear and sing this carol this season, think about the words and how they apply to the Christmas story, "...the Lord is come!" We should rejoice! Remember the reason Jesus came, to save the world. Be ready because He is coming again! What a glorious day THAT will be when the whole earth celebrates His appearing!

Something to think about

Read slowly through the hymn below and in each verse note the reason for joy.
  • What is the response to be upon hearing the news?
  • How should it affect the way we live?
Describe in your own words what you believe the meaning of the last verse is.

Joy to the World

Joy to the world, the Lord is come!
Let earth receive her King;
Let every heart prepare Him room,
And Heaven and nature sing,
And Heaven and nature sing,
And Heaven, and Heaven, and nature sing.

Joy to the earth, the Savior reigns!
Let men their songs employ;
While fields and floods, rocks, hills and plains
Repeat the sounding joy,
Repeat the sounding joy,
Repeat, repeat, the sounding joy.

No more let sins and sorrows grow,
Nor thorns infest the ground;
He comes to make His blessings flow
Far as the curse is found,
Far as the curse is found,
Far as, far as, the curse is found.

He rules the world with truth and grace,
And makes the nations prove
The glories of His righteousness,
And wonders of His love,
And wonders of His love,
And wonders, wonders, of His love.

Music - Lowell Mason, adapted from Handel, Words - Isaac Watts 1839.
Public Domain

In every corner of the globe, Christ sets the captive free and puts a song in lonely hearts. He reigns as king in the lives of men. And He can bring joy to you if you really believe the message, "Joy to the world, the Lord is come."

When they saw the star, they rejoiced exceedingly with great joy.
– Matthew 2:10

Devotional Week Three - Thursday

DAILY DEVOTIONALS - WEEK THREE

Friday

God does extraordinary things through ordinary people!

...that you may proclaim the excellencies of him who called you out of darkness into his marvelous light. - 1 Peter 2:9

Jesus' birth was announced first to the shepherds, an unlikely group to receive such an important announcement. It didn't come to the religious leaders of the day; it came to those of no significance.

Do you ever think that God isn't able to use you? Maybe you feel that you aren't very gifted or talented. Maybe you feel just like an ordinary person. Or maybe you feel less than ordinary and that you will never be able to be used in a significant way for the Lord.

Historically God has chosen ordinary people to do extraordinary things.
- Moses was a shepherd, God called him to deliver a nation.
- David was a shepherd boy who defeated Goliath and became the king of Israel.
- Nehemiah was a cupbearer and God called him to rebuild the walls around Jerusalem.
- Mary was a young girl when God called her to be the mother of the Messiah.
- Peter was a fisherman, Jesus called him to establish the church.

These were ordinary men and women just like you and me.

God uses people from all walks of life and those who have only their faithfulness and willingness to say, "Yes Lord," to spread the good news of His Son. God chose to use the shepherds to describe how great His love for us is.

This week as we think about Advent, we discover that God does extraordinary things through ordinary people. God chose insignificant, outcasts of the day to reveal His magnificence and He is still doing it today!

Daily Bible reading
John 1:12
Matthew 6:26-33
1 Corinthians 1:26-30

Something to think about

No matter what stage of life you are in, no matter what obstacles you face, what you're lacking in skills, education or gifting, God desires to use you in extraordinary ways to expand His Kingdom! When God calls, keep a vertical focus! When we focus on the horizontal (what we have or don't have, what others say about us, what we say to ourselves etc.), we will miss out on God sized opportunities and seeing God do extraordinary things in and through us.

What has God called you to? Whatever it is, it's something wonderful and extraordinary! Are you willing to do extraordinary things? If there is any hesitation at all, all you have to do is say, "Yes Lord" and take the next step!

God reminds us,
...as you have done it to the least of these, you have done it to me!
– Matthew 25:45

DAILY DEVOTIONALS - WEEK THREE

Saturday

Hope was born and He brought with Him joy, peace and power!

God sent the angels to announce the birth not to the important and the elite, but to the outcasts of society, men who were without hope. As they looked into the face of the baby, they realized that Hope had been born for them! Men who were outcasts, on the fringe of society and insignificant, now found hope and they were filled with joy and peace!

They could not stop telling everyone the good news they had heard and seen.

The prophet Isaiah said, "The root of Jesse will come, even he who arises to rule the Gentiles, in him will the Gentiles hope." (Isaiah 11:10) May the God of hope fill you with all joy and peace in believing, so that by the power of the Holy Spirit you may abound in hope.

Before coming to Christ, we were without hope. But, now in Christ we have hope! As a believer we are never without hope! But that is not all. As we live a life of surrender to Christ, we also have joy, peace and power! What more could you hope for?

However, there are times when life seems hopeless. In those times it is important that you

- Stop and pray. Ask God to show you what is hindering your joy and peace. When He does, confess it as sin and do whatever it takes to remove the barrier. But also, don't put God in a box of your own making. In other words realize that His ways are not our ways and ask Him to bring your desires in line with His.
- Believe! Believe that God is a good Father, that He loves you, and that He will do what He said He would do! When you believe, you will be

filled with peace!

- Remember the Holy Spirit will empower and strengthen you. You are not in this alone! God has set you up to succeed in the plans and purposes He has for your life.

Daily Bible reading
Romans 15:12-13
Ephesians 2:12
1 Peter 1:3
Hebrew11:1
Philippians 4:7

Something to think about

God is the God of hope and the very foundation on which our hope is built. He is both the object and the author of our hope. When we trust in God by the power of the Holy Spirit, we experience

- **Joy**, which comes as we anticipate seeing our hopes fulfilled. Much like the excitement of a child on Christmas morning.
- **Peace** which comes from the assurance that God will do what He said He would do.

Joy is the emotional result of hope.
Peace is the emotional result of faith.

+ Take time today to evaluate your emotional health by answering the following questions.
- What or Who is your hope fastened to? Explain your answer.
- When life is seemingly spinning out of control do you trust God or do you simply give him lip service? Don't answer to quickly! Ask the Lord to show you!
- From what you read, what two things may be indicators of misplaced hope?
- Can you think of a time or times in your life where you lacked joy or peace?
Describe the circumstance and how you responded.
How would you handle it in the future?

Our hope is based on knowing God will do what He said He would do. And so we wait expectantly knowing that Jesus is coming back!!!

May the God of hope fill you with all joy and peace in believing, so that by the power of the Holy Spirit you may abound in hope this Advent season and every day!

Devotional Week Three - Saturday

FOURTH SUNDAY OF ADVENT

The Angel's Candle - Love

Do not be afraid; for behold, I bring you good news of great joy which will be for all the people; for today in the city of David there has been born for you a Savior, who is Christ the Lord. - Luke 2:10-11

Today we light the candle for the fourth Sunday of Advent. Each week we light the candles of the previous weeks and then the candle for the current week. As the candles are illuminated, and the room is flooded with light, there is an air of anticipation and excitement for the coming of the Light of the world! In preparation for celebrating this final Sunday before Christmas, we light the candles of Hope, Peace and Joy. As we light the fourth candle, the Angel Candle, we celebrate the Angel's message of love, which they have waited thousands of years to deliver! In doing so we are reminded that God sent His only Son to earth to save us, because He loves us!

We light this candle heralding the coming of the Light of God into the world. With the coming of this Light there is love!

For God so loved the world, that he gave his only Son, that whoever believes
in him should not perish but have eternal life. For God did not send
his Son into the world to condemn the world, but in order that
the world might be saved through him.
John 3:16-17

What do you think of when you think of angels?

For most of us we probably think of the illustrations we have seen in art and in the movies. You might be thinking of Clarence in "It's A Wonderful Life" or maybe chubby little cherubs with curly hair and stubby wings. Often people think of friends or loved ones, especially children, who have died. At a child's funeral you sometimes hear a grieving parent say God called one of His angels home. It is interesting that those sorts of angelic figures exist in our culture. But, they are not the angels of Scripture.

What the Bible says
The Bible tells us that the angels were created for one reason, to do God's will. To put it another way, they were created to be God's instruments or agents to carry out His work. In fact, the word "angel" actually means "messenger" or "agent." The Bible says, "Praise the Lord, you His angels, you mighty ones who do His bidding, who obey His word." (Psalm 103:20)

Just as the angels are largely unseen by us, so also is their work. It's quite possible that when we get to heaven, we will be amazed to discover all the things God did through His angels —including their protection over us in times of danger. (This includes not only physical danger, but moral and spiritual danger, as well.) The Bible says, "For He will command His angels concerning you to guard you in all your ways." (Psalm 91:11)

Angels have a recurring role not only in the Christmas narrative, but also throughout the entire Bible.

Let's take a look at some of the roles angels have played.

Executors of God's judgment
Because of the Assyrian siege of Jerusalem, the angel of the LORD struck down 185,000 in the Assyrian camp in order to break the siege. (Isaiah 37:33-37)

It was two angels, who brought judgment to Sodom and Gomorrah. And much later, when Nebuchadnezzar's pride got the best of him, it was an angel that declared his kingship would be cut down like a tree. (Daniel 4:13-17)

These are not chubby cherubs but terrifying beings who have authority to execute the judgment of God.

Our help in times of trouble

Angels shut up the mouths of lions (Daniel 6) and opened prison doors. (Acts 12) They are sent to help and protect the children of God.

God's Messengers

Serving as God's messengers is one of the main tasks of angels in the Bible. Often when they appeared, the first words they said were "Do not be afraid!" Their sudden appearance in the Bible seems to have been terrifying. Men fainted and women cried when they realized they were talking with an angel.

The angel Gabriel was God's mouthpiece, first to Zacharias that he would father a son, whom he was to name John, and who would be the forerunner of the Messiah. (Luke 1:8-20) Then to Joseph and Mary to tell them Mary would give birth to the Messiah, God's plan for them and even answered their questions. (Luke 1:26-38, Matthew 1:20-25)

Then one quiet evening the sky SUDDENLY exploded with light, the glory of God surrounded a group of shepherds just outside Bethlehem, and an angel appeared announcing the birth of Jesus, followed by a choir of angels singing "Glory to God in the highest, and on earth peace among those with whom He is pleased!" (Luke 2:8-14)

The angelic host proclaimed the birth of the Savior, the Messiah (Christ), the Lord.

The fourth candle reminds us that on that first Christmas day, the angels came to declare that there is a new King in this world, one whose rule will never end. This kingdom is both a present and future reality. He is King and He will always be King. As Christians we live in the kingdom of this world as citizens of the Kingdom of the coming world. That is the message of the angels to everyone who will listen.

We aren't to worship the angels or pay too much attention to them, Christ alone is our living hope. Their role is to magnify the greatness of Jesus Christ, worshipping and serving Him, ministering in the lives of believers so that when we look at the work of angels, our gaze continues to Jesus, to dwell on Him and His great glory!

God so Loved the World

Christmas is the perfect time to focus on LOVE! It is said that the one question every person longs to have answered is "Am I loved?" The desire to be loved is common to us all despite our religion, race or nationality. How ironic is it that often the emotions caused by the lack of love in one's life are often heightened during the Christmas season? Yet it is a time when many are open to conversations they might not willingly have at other times.

Don't let the busyness of the season distract you from the needs of those around you! Ask God to keep you sensitive to those He brings into your path each day (neighbors, cashiers, waitresses, etc.) Be alert to, and prepared for those God opportunities to enter into conversations, so that you can share the greatest gift of all this Christmas!

What hope, peace, joy, and love we should feel when we deeply consider the message of the angel, "I bring you good news of great joy…" that Jesus came to this world He created to provide a way for us to be reunited with God, our Creator. He did this willingly, knowing what He would endure. He loves us so much that He did what only He could do. Because of that, we can rejoice…

Daily Bible reading

Luke 2:8–14
Daniel 4:13-17
Isaiah 37:36
Luke 1:8-20
Luke 1:26-38
Matthew 1:20-25

Something to think about

From the beginning God had a plan. On the first day of Creation God spoke light into the darkness! The earth was full of God's peace, the kind of peace in which everything works according to God's plan. The world was made for man with everything we could ever need or want, to live joyfully in the presence of our Creator. We would worship God by loving Him and one another forever. The angels were also there at creation and shouted for joy! (Job 38:4,7)

But one day Adam and Eve rejected God's rule over them. We refer to their rebellious choice as "the Fall." Because they represented all of mankind, their action affects us too. Through our attitudes and actions we too have declared ourselves to be God's enemies. The result of rejecting God's rule over us is that we are dead spiritually, will die physically.

Thankfully, even though our Creator hates our sin and we all deserve death, there is good news! He is determined to turn the evil and suffering we have caused into good that will ultimately be for His glory. God loves you and has a plan for you, which is a part of His master plan for redeeming His world and rescuing sinners!

The first Christmas day changed the world. On that day hope was born! God tucked Himself up under the heart of a young virgin in the form of a tiny baby. This baby Jesus, God Himself, had come to renew the world and restore His people. This redemption came with a price, the death and resurrection of Jesus. It was a price that Jesus was aware of, but because of God's great love for us, He chose to come anyway. Light stepped into darkness and that Light continues to cover the darkness today!

But, the story doesn't end with redemption. God promised to renew the whole world. The Bible gives us a glimpse into this glorious future. This restoration will take place in two ways. Christ will return to judge sin and evil. He will usher in righteousness and peace. God will remove evil from the world once and for all! That same light that God spoke into the darkness at Creation, and which covered the darkness until His return, will be the Light of His eternal Kingdom forever and ever.

Christmas is intensely personal. Don't miss this! It is the day Christians celebrate the birth of Jesus, the one who saves His people from their sins. Have you bowed the knee, have you surrendered your life to become a member of His kingdom? If you have never surrendered your life to Christ, what better time could there possibly be than now? Bow your head, and in prayer ask God to forgive you of your sins and allow Him to have the authority in your life.

If you are reading this and you gave your life to Christ, you need to let someone know. Talk to a pastor, small group leader or another believer. They will pray with you and for you and point you in the right direction.

Thank God for His love for you—a love so deep that He sent His Son to die for your sins, and now sends His angels to watch over you.

Fourth Sunday Journal

DAILY DEVOTIONALS - WEEK FOUR

Monday

Hope is born!

The angel said to them, "Fear not, for behold, I bring you good news of great joy that will be for all the people. For unto you is born this day in the city of David a Savior, who is Christ the Lord. - Luke 2:10-11

The great day has arrived! Mary has given birth to her firstborn son, Jesus. That night, just outside Bethlehem, shepherds were keeping watch over their flocks. Suddenly the sky was ablaze with the glory of the Lord and an angel of the Lord appeared to them! The shepherds were terrified!

The angel's message was comforting. "Don't be afraid." This was the same message the angel gave to Zechariah and to Mary. (Luke 1:13, 30) The rest of the message was that the long-awaited Savior, Christ the Lord, was born. This was good news of great joy that was for ALL people, not just the Jews. And the Savior was born in Bethlehem, exactly where the prophets said He would be born.

The announcement was that the long-awaited hope, for Israel and all people, was born! God had sent a Savior to meet man's greatest need. It was a message full of hope, peace, joy and love that the shepherds preached to everyone they saw!

On this day everything changed! Messiah has come! This day was the beginning of the new creation!

Daily Bible reading
Luke 2:8-12
Luke 1:13, 30

Something to think about

Remember God had a plan from the beginning, now God's plan of redemption is beginning to unfold. Both the shepherds and the angels were part of that plan. The angels did what angels do, they delivered God's message to the shepherds that Hope is born! The shepherds responded by sharing the good news with everyone they saw.

Just as God had a plan from the beginning, and the angels and shepherds were part of executing that plan, so are we! The angels brought the message of redemption to the shepherds, who shared the gospel message with everyone they saw. We too have been given the gospel to share with those whom God brings into our life.

What about you? Have you received the message of hope? If so, what have you done with it? Have you shared it with everyone God brings into your life? Or, have you kept it to yourself?

Unless we understand that God's purpose for us is to share the gospel, and plan for, pray over, prepare, and purpose to watch for the opportunity to share – IT WON'T HAPPEN. Planning takes time and discipline, but what great joy will be seen in the faces of the hopeless when you bring them a message of hope.

Today make a plan and write it down. If you don't know where to start, begin with prayer, then write out the gospel message in a way that is easy for you to share.
- Now that you have written it out, practice it. When you are getting ready for the day share the gospel. When you are driving down the road share the gospel. When you are walking, running or working out, share the gospel.
- Pray, asking God to show you who needs to hear the gospel today.
- Purpose ahead of time to speak to whomever God brings your way.
- When God gives you a name or shows you someone to speak to just obey, and watch for Him to give you an opportunity to share the gospel with them.
- Don't worry if you can't "remember it exactly." The Holy Spirit will empower you to do it.

Remember, you are only responsible for the delivery. God is responsible for the result!

Devotional Week Four - Monday

DAILY DEVOTIONALS - WEEK FOUR

Tuesday

Jesus' birth drew angels from heaven.

Suddenly there was with the angel a multitude of the heavenly host praising God and saying, "Glory to God in the highest, and on earth peace among those with whom He is pleased! – Luke 2:13-14

When the first angel finished his message, the sky exploded and heaven invaded the earth at the crux of God's redemptive plan. An angelic choir sang praises to God and glorified His name.

Praise is the proper response to God's grace, not only of the believer but all of God's creation. (Psalm 148:1-4)

The angels first sang at Creation (Job 38:7), and now they are singing at the beginning of the new creation!

For the first time in centuries, the glory of God returned to earth. God's glory had dwelt in the tabernacle (Exodus 40:34) and in the temple (2 Chronicles 7:1-3) but had departed because of Israel's sin. Now God's glory was returning to earth in the person of God's Son. (John 1:14)

Daily Bible reading
Psalm 148:1-4
Job 38:7
Exodus 40:34-38
2 Chronicles 7:1-3
John 1:14

Something to think about

One can only imagine how amazed the angels were at the sight of God Himself tucked up inside the body of this tiny baby.

The angels had been waiting for the next part of God's plan to unfold for a very long time! And when it did, the heavens exploded with the sound of angel voices and the glory of the Lord lit up the night sky!

Why should we care what these angels say at Messiah's birth? What is it about them that make them reliable sources to listen to? They came from the very presence of God in heaven to announce the Savior's birth. It was the angels who heralded the good news to those on earth. It was the angels who taught us all we know about Jesus' birth.

Ask yourself the following questions and write the answers out.
- What have I learned about Jesus and His birth? (Luke 1:8-38, Matthew 1:20-25)
- Do I share their joy at the birth of Jesus? Do others see that joy in me? If not, why not?
- In what ways do I praise God?
- How do I glorify His name?

Devotional Week Four - Tuesday

DAILY DEVOTIONALS - WEEK FOUR

Wednesday

Hark! the Herald Angels Sing.

One of the things I love about Christmas is the music. I'm talking about the good, old-fashioned Christmas Carols. Many of us have sung these same songs year after year until they are a part of us, and we sing without even thinking about it.

A few years ago during church, I noticed the lyrics on the screen and began to read them. Soon I became so captivated by them I stopped singing. It was as though suddenly they were lifted from the screen and embedded in my heart. I looked around me at the people singing and wondered if those singing had ever given pause to what they were saying. I began to realize that the gospel is being proclaimed year after year, in churches, schools, public auditorium's and even shopping malls, to the unsuspecting!

As we've already seen, in previous weeks, many of the carols we sing are rich in their theology, and "Hark! The Herald Angels Sing" is no exception. Charles Wesley, an English Methodist leader and hymn writer, wrote more than 8,000 hymns! He wrote this carol in 1739, about one year after his conversion, to be read on Christmas Day. He doesn't simply tell the story of Jesus' birth, rather he tells us the entire gospel story.

The first stanza is telling us to listen carefully to the angels who are announcing the birth of the King. The next stanza talks about Jesus' remarkable birth through a young virgin. The very last stanza tells us three reasons why Jesus was born.

For over 250 years, the gospel infused hymn "Hark, the Herald Angels Sing" has been pointing people to the Savior. However, you may have wondered, like me, what in the world does "Hark the Herald" mean and what about a couple of those other phrases? In old English "Hark" means, listen or pay attention; "Herald" means messenger, someone who makes an important announcement. Another phrase that's confusing is "Mild he lays his glory by." It refers to Christ's willingness to lay aside the glory of heaven to become flesh and become one of us. Then there is, "Late in time behold him come," which means, that after many hundreds of years of His people waiting, at God's appointed time He came.

Have you paid attention to what the messenger is saying?

Daily Bible reading
Luke 2:14
2 Corinthians 5:19
Galatians 4:4
John 1:14
Isaiah 9:6
Malachi 4:2
Philippians 2:5-11
1 Peter 1:3

Something to think about

Read or sing "Hark! the Herald Angels Sing" aloud.

Write the main subject of each stanza beside it.

Read through the song again. This time mark every reference to the newborn King and all his synonyms with a cross.

Make a list of all you learn about this newborn King. Don't forget to add any new names you learned for Jesus to your list in the back of the book.

Hark! the Herald Angels Sing

Hark! the herald angels sing
"Glory to the newborn King!
Peace on earth and mercy mild,
God and sinners reconciled"
Joyful, all ye nations rise
Join the triumph of the skies
With the angelic host proclaim:
"Christ is born in Bethlehem"
Hark! The herald angels sing
"Glory to the newborn King!"

Christ by highest heav'n adored
Christ the everlasting Lord!
Late in time behold Him come
Offspring of a Virgin's womb
Veiled in flesh the Godhead see
Hail the incarnate Deity
Pleased as man with man to dwell
Jesus, our Emmanuel
Hark! The herald angels sing
"Glory to the newborn King!"

Hail the heav'n-born Prince of Peace!
Hail the Son of Righteousness!
Light and life to all He brings
Ris'n with healing in His wings
Mild He lays His glory by
Born that man no more may die
Born to raise the sons of earth
Born to give them second birth
Hark! The herald angels sing
"Glory to the newborn King!"

Author: Charles Wesley (1739) Tune: MENDELSSOHN
Public Domain

Think about it, God's redemption of His people is all about God's glory. We can look at this story of Christ's coming into the world, and we can still be man-centered about it by thinking it is all about us. But, the angels are reminding us that even as Jesus comes to earth to rescue men and women, boys and girls, it's all about God's glory!

As you sing carols this Christmas, take the time to think about the message of the songs and what they mean. Consider the words you are singing and the truths they proclaim about the Savior you are worshiping. Pray for those around you as they too sing, that the words will invade their hearts. Use this song as an opportunity to discuss it and share the gospel.

DAILY DEVOTIONALS - WEEK FOUR

Thursday

Love gives.

For God so loved the world, that he gave his only Son, that whoever believes in him should not perish but have eternal life. For God did not send his Son into the world to condemn the world, but in order that the world might be saved through him. - John 3:16-17

 Another thing I LOVE about Christmas is the giving and receiving of gifts. I love thinking about and searching for the perfect gift, one that will bring great joy to the recipient as well as a sense of how much they are loved. I love to watch them unwrap the package with anticipation of what might be inside, hear the ooohs and ahhhs, and see the sparkle of delight in their eyes when the gift is unveiled!

The Angel's message reminds us that everything God does is because of His great love for people. God's love is not limited to a few or just one people group. His gift is for the whole world. God knew that the best gift He could give us was not tangible.

The greatest need people have is to be loved unconditionally. God knew the only way that need could be met was for someone to love them right where they were, with no strings attached. God alone could do that. But there was a problem; there was a barrier between God and us that needed to be removed. It was a barrier created by our own sin and rebellion.

So, God showed just how much He loves the world, by giving His most priceless gift – His only Son, so that man may have a new life, eternal life, from now and forever. Only Christ can overcome the sin that separates us from God. It is a gift simply to be received, not earned. (John 1:12-13) A person receives it by believing and trusting in Christ.

God's purpose in sending His Son is salvation, not condemnation. God does not delight in the death of the wicked. (Ezekiel 18:23, 32) God's greatest desire is that everyone would be saved. (1 Timothy 2:4, 2 Peter 3:9)

Daily Bible reading
John 1:12-13, 3:16-18
Romans 8:3, 32
1 John 4:9
Ezekiel 18:23, 32
1 Timothy 2:4
2 Peter 3:9

Something to think about

It was because of love that God created man in the first place. Why? Because love needs people to love! In other words, love always requires tangible expression. It was because of this love that God put a plan in place to rescue us from the destructive path we chose with our free will. Love sent Jesus into our world. Hope was born.

Make this your prayer today

Father, thank you for the gift of Your Son! Please forgive me for the times I have failed to love or to follow through on my attempts at love. Please help me to feel Your love and consistently act on it. Lord, I want to give the gift of Your Son to those You bring my way. Give me eyes to see the needs of those around me, and how I can love them in a tangible way. So that, they will see Your love through me and in doing so give me an open door to share the gospel with them. Amen.

DAILY DEVOTIONALS - WEEK FOUR

Friday

Loving God by Loving People

When we really understand this amazing gift God has given us, we can't help but want to love Him back! We've seen that love requires a tangible expression. God knew that man's greatest need was to be loved unconditionally, so He chose His gift accordingly. But what is the best gift we can give God that He doesn't already have?

God's greatest desire is that everyone would be saved! But we can't save them, only God can. So what is the best gift we can give God? It is love! We received God's gift of love, not so that we keep it to ourselves, but so that we can give God's love to others!

Today there is a lot of hatred in a world full of people looking for unconditional love. If we are called to be God's hands and feet, leading people to reconciliation with Him, love is our most powerful vehicle. We are to love God and love people. So, how do we do that? By being agents of God, loving and showing concern for people and their well being. If they can see God's love in us, they will be drawn to us, and we can point them to Him.

The result of loving God is that you will love people. And loving people is the way to show the world that you love God. We are called to be a light shining in the darkness. Because hope was born in us, we should be a people offering hope to a hopeless world.

Daily Bible reading
Leviticus 19:18
Luke 6:27-28, 10:30-37
Acts 7:54-60
James 2:15-16

Something to think about

As believers, the Holy Spirit resides in us. Therefore, we should be the expression of the love of God to others. It is not simply telling others "I love you." It must be demonstrated by meeting their needs. It would have been a terrible thing if God had simply said that He loved the world, and yet did not send His Son to redeem mankind. Or if He said He forgave us, but then refused to have anything to do with us.

Don't just say you love someone; prove it! Loving others with God's love often involves a sacrifice of time, emotions, possessions, and more. But in light of the sacrifice God made for us by sending His Son, that first Christmas morning, our choice to love others demonstrates our gratefulness to Him and will be a sacrifice well worth making. Because God loved us, we should love the people He has placed in our lives. Loving God and loving people should define our entire life.

How do you love the people around you, including the ones who make you uncomfortable? Ask God to give you eyes to see their needs and the ability to meet them. Then go out and lavish them in God's love.

Let your light shine before men, so that they may see your good works
and give glory to your Father who is in heaven. - Matthew 5:16

DAILY DEVOTIONALS - WEEK FOUR

Saturday

To all who did receive Him, who believed in His name (have faith in Christ), He gave the right to become children of God – John 1:12

To believe in His name is to acknowledge that Jesus is who the Scriptures say He is, and to surrender fully to Him, so that He can be all of that to us. By believing in Christ's name, we receive Him as a gift from God. In doing so, we also must receive His teaching as true and good, His law as just and holy, and we must receive His grace and love as the ruling principles of our love and actions.

Daily Bible reading
John 1:1-18

Something to think about

God's Christmas tree is the cross. This is where God hung His gift—His only son—for you. Have you received God's gift or is it still sitting there unopened? Don't open man's gifts and miss the gift of eternal life! Today is the day of salvation!!!!!

Devotional Week Four - Saturday

CHRISTMAS DAY

The Greatest Gift of All, The Birth of Jesus Christ

The Jesus Candle

Finally, we light the fifth candle of Advent. This candle is called the Jesus candle, it is lit on either Christmas Eve or Christmas Day to remind Christians of the light Jesus brings to the world.

As I've said earlier there are so many things I love about Christmas, lights, decorations, parties, presents and I especially love Advent and the daily reminders to keep me focused on the reason we celebrate. Today is the day we've been waiting to celebrate, the Greatest Gift of All, the Birth of Jesus Christ!

Gifts come in a variety of sizes and packaging. Some come clenched in the grubby hands of a child, some in the bag they were bought in, others arrive in pretty bags or boxes wrapped in brightly colored paper surrounded by ribbon and topped with bows. It seems the more special or valuable the gift, the more exquisite the packaging!

The presentation is important and depends completely on the giver of the gift. Little children will ask you to close your eyes, as they hide their gift behind their back, and then to open them as they present their treasure. Hopeful suitors will kneel before their lady, after carefully considering the venue, to present the engagement ring prior to their proposal.

Some gifts are expected and some are a complete surprise!

God's gift to us was the greatest gift one can receive. However, to almost everyone it was a complete surprise! Even though the prophets had spoken of the coming Messiah, no one expected the Creator to come as one created, a baby who had been tucked up under the heart of His mother Mary.

Think about that gift. Baby Jesus wasn't born in a fancy venue such as a palace. He was born in a stable, He came in the humblest of wrappings, swaddling clothes, and was laid in a feed trough. What an invaluable sacrifice God made because of the great love He had for the whole world. God's gift to humanity, redemption and eternal life through His Son, Jesus Christ, came in the simplest and humblest of wrappings.

It wasn't a gift we deserved, God gave us His gift when we were His enemies. The Bible tells us, "God shows His love for us in that while we were still sinners, Christ died for us." (Romans 5:8) It was part of God's plan from the very beginning! The Bible also tells us that He was slain from the foundation of the world. (Revelation 13:8) The gift that God has given to us was the most sacrificial thing He could have possibly offered.

Christmas isn't about the gifts you have under your tree, or the ones you have given to others. Those things will all be gone one day. Christmas is all about the gift of eternal life we have been given through God's Son, Jesus Christ. Life, in the here and now, is about knowing the God who created you and who gave you the greatest gift you will ever receive and making Him known to all those you come in contact with.

Most of the world, in Jesus' day, didn't realize just how great a gift they had been given. Today most people still don't, including many believers. As you examine this gift carefully, you realize how valuable a gift it actually is. This week we are going to take a look at some of the names of Jesus and hopefully come to a deeper understanding of just how great a gift we have in Jesus.

Daily Bible reading
Romans 5

Christmas Day Journal

DAILY DEVOTIONALS - CHRISTMAS WEEK

Day 1

Who is Baby Jesus?

During the four weeks leading up to Christmas day our focus has been on the birth of Jesus. We began by looking at Matthew and Luke's accounts of the birth narratives, and the fulfilling of Old Testament prophesies concerning the Messiah. Shepherds watching their flocks, wise men, a star, angels and of course manger scenes. The stuff all good Christmas plays are made of.

Today we are going to the gospel of John, focusing on John 1:1-18, looking further back than the birth narratives, to get a better understanding of just who this baby is and just how great of a gift we have in Him.

Today we're doing something a little different. We are going to engage the Word in a way that will slow us down and enable us to see exactly Who this baby is. We don't want to miss it! It's not going to be hard, but it will take some time. The insights will be mind-boggling!

Follow the instructions, and discover just
Who the Baby Jesus is for yourself!

We are going to be marking words in this exercise. If you want, you can do it directly in your Bible. If you don't want to write in your Bible, you can print out John 1:1-8, double-spaced with wide margins (so you can take notes) and mark on that.

+ Make your lists on the page where you listed Jesus' Names and Character Traits, in previous weeks.
   • Read John 1: 1-18 and circle Word, including the pronouns (words, which refer to the Word). As an example: In the beginning was

the Word, and the Word was with God, and the Word was God.
Did you notice any synonyms (a word having a meaning that is the same as or very similar) for Word?

- Read John1: 1-18 again, and circle any synonyms, just as you did Word.
  What did you learn about the Word? (Make a list of all that you learned about the Word.)
  According to verse 1, who is "He" and how is "He" described?
  What does verse 14 teach about the Word?

- Read verses 14 through 18 and draw a square around the phrase: grace and truth.
  According to verse 14, what are the characteristics of the Word?
  How is Jesus described in verse 18?
  What difference does it make in your life that Jesus is God?

Daily Bible reading
John 15:13
Jude 1:25
2 Timothy 1:9
Colossians 1:16-19

Something to think about

Did you notice how far back John went? He went all the way back before Creation to eternity, because he wants us to understand just who this baby is! The baby in the manger, whom we celebrate, is eternal and the Creator of all things! John begins his gospel by showing that Jesus, the Christ, the Son of God, existed before time … this is baby Jesus!

The more we examine the Word, the more we understand how great a gift we've been given. The wonder of it all!

DAILY DEVOTIONALS - CHRISTMAS WEEK

Day 2

Jesus is God's plan for a promised deliverer! He is our rescuer!

She will bear a son, and you shall call his name Jesus, for he will save his people from their sins. - Matthew 1:21

An angel appeared to Joseph in a dream and explained Mary's pregnancy. At the same time the angel told Joseph the baby would be a boy and to name him Jesus, because He would save His people from their sins.

Actually, the baby boy was given two names, Jesus and Immanuel. Jesus, revealed His mission, to "save His people from their sins." Immanuel revealed who He was in that redemptive mission, "God is with us" to save and also to judge.

Jesus means Savior, salvation is the purpose of His mission here on earth. His death and resurrection are the foundation of our salvation. As the Savior, Jesus is God's plan for a promised deliverer, who rescues man from sin and death into immortality and life. Jesus is the hope of the believer.

Jesus, there is no other name under heaven by which we must be saved.
– Acts 4:12

Daily Bible reading
Matthew 1:18-25
Acts 13:23-25
Titus 2:11-14, 3:4-8
Philippians 3:20-21

Something to think about

God's plan from the very beginning was that Jesus would come to rescue His people from sin and death. Jesus' first coming, His death, burial and resurrection accomplished His purpose for coming. Because of salvation we have the power to overcome sin and have hope for the future. This is what separates us from the world.

The way others know we are God's people is by the way we live! We are to do life in such a way that there is no question in the minds of all who are watching that we are God's children. We can say we are a believer all day long, but if we are not living in obedience to God's Word and instead live like everyone else in the world, we have no evidence that we are the children of God. From the beginning God made a distinction between light and darkness, His chosen people the Jews, and the nations surrounding them, and now believers and unbelievers. John tells us in 1 John 3:10 that the children of God and the children of the devil are obvious.

Does your walk and your talk match who you say you are? At home, in public and at church?

✳ Self Evaluation: When others look at your lifestyle what do they see? List below what distinguishes you as a child of God other than your profession or church attendance.

If your friends, family, co-workers etc. were asked if you were a Christian what would they say? What is the evidence they would point to?

Is there anything in your life that may be clouding the vision of those who are watching? Take time today and ask God to show you anything that may be a distraction to them. If He does, write it down. Pray and confess it. Do whatever it takes to get rid of it!

Remember grace is greater than all of your sins!

DAILY DEVOTIONALS - CHRISTMAS WEEK

Day 3

Immanuel – God is with us

Behold, the virgin shall conceive and bear a son, and shall call his name Immanuel. - Isaiah 7:14

The essence of this passage and event in history is not merely that a baby was born, rather that God became a baby! God was wrapped in swaddling cloths lying in the manger. Isaiah prophesied, "For to us a child is born, to us a son is given..." (Isaiah 9:6) Did you notice what Isaiah said? He said that the child is born, but the Son is given. Isaiah used a contrast to make the point because the Son existed before the child was born. The virgin gave birth to a child, but the child existed before the virgin ever got pregnant. Therefore, the Son was given, not born.

Not only did Jesus come to do the Father's will, but He came to put God on display to all who were watching, so that we would know what it is like to have God with us. Jesus Himself said, "Whoever has seen me has seen the Father." (John 14:9)

> ### *Daily Bible reading*
> Hebrews 1:3, 10:5-7
> Colossians 1:15
> John 1:1-18

Something to think about

Everywhere you turn people are in crisis. Many are in the hardest situations they have ever faced. The Bible says He gives us a future and a hope. Life may be so overwhelming we may not be able to see it, we may not even be aware of His Presence on the most difficult days. But He hasn't abandoned us, and He never will.

In those times it is important to keep a vertical focus, remembering the gift of Jesus Christ, Immanuel, not just at Christmas but also all year long! In both seasons of celebration and in seasons of brokenness, He's still with us. Even when it looks like God is nowhere around, He is with you! Realizing He is ever present in your life affords you the power to accomplish His plan and purposes for you.

If Jesus came to put God on display so that we would know what it is like to have God with us, and Jesus lives in us, how should we live in order that all who are watching would know God?

How does knowing and understanding God as Immanuel, bring hope when you are walking through difficult circumstances? How will that affect those who are watching?

Devotional Week Christmas - Day 3

Day 4

The Lord our righteousness

Behold, the days are coming, declares the LORD, when I will raise up for David a righteous Branch, and he shall reign as king and deal wisely, and shall execute justice and righteousness in the land. In his days Judah will be saved, and Israel will dwell securely. And this is the name by which he will be called: 'The LORD is our righteousness.' - Jeremiah 23:5-6

Judah had refused to listen to God's Words and walked in the stubbornness of their hearts. They had chased after other gods. (Jeremiah 13:10) The whole nation walked in their own ways and corrupted themselves. Except for a very small remnant, they did what was evil in the sight of the Lord.

This corruption was at the top, even polluting the priesthood. God could no longer accept them and must call their sins to account. (Jeremiah 14:10) Nothing short of repentance could stop it. (Jeremiah 15:5-11) However, when confronted, the people of Judah replied,

> *That is hopeless! We will follow our own plans, and will every one act according to the stubbornness of his evil heart. (Jeremiah 18:12).*

They believed they were too far gone, without hope.

Immanuel, it's a name of hope for those who have given up hope. It's a name of life for those who can see only death and hopelessness.

In order to dwell with God we must be righteous. To be righteous is to do what God says is right, to live according to His standards. (Romans 3:10-12, 23) The problem is we cannot live according to God's standards. Our hearts are so sin sick that we can't even begin to live in a way that pleases God without Jesus. The good news is that Hope was born, and His name is the Lord Our Righteousness, Jesus!

Daily Bible reading
Romans 3:10-12, 23
Jeremiah 31:33-34; 32:40
Ezekiel 36:26-27

Something to think about

✴ Go back and read Jeremiah 23:5-6 (above) and answer the following questions:
- What is the Lord going to do for His people according to verse 5?
- Make a list of all you learn about this Righteous Branch in your journal.
- Who do you think this Righteous Branch is?

Have you ever felt hopeless? Have you ever thought that your sin was too great, your heart too dark, that you were so far beyond hope to ever be right with God? Well there is good news! The Lord our Righteousness is a name of hope for those who have given up hope! It's a name of life for those who can only see death. It's a radiant beacon cutting through the darkness pointing the way to eternal life.

A new covenant and a new heart will come because of a righteous Branch named, the Lord Our Righteousness. At the cross,

> *God made Him to be sin who knew no sin, so that in Him we might become the righteousness of God. (2 Corinthians 5:21)*

> *...the righteousness of God through faith in Jesus Christ for all who believe. (Romans 3:22)*

You can be right with God!

Devotional Week Christmas - Day 4

DAILY DEVOTIONALS - CHRISTMAS WEEK

Day 5

Jesus is the Light of the world!

Jesus spoke to them, saying, "I am the light of the world. Whoever follows me will not walk in darkness, but will have the light of life. - John 8:12

The light of the candles itself becomes an important image of the season. The light reminds us that,

- Jesus is the light of the world that comes into the darkness of our lives to bring new life, and hope.
- We are called to be a light to the world reflecting the light of God's grace to others. (Isaiah 42:6)

The Creator of the heavens and the earth promised His Servant (Jesus) that He had been called to perform God's gospel plan for the world. Because the Lord would take hold of the Servant's hand, He would be empowered to carry out God's plan.

Because of His death and resurrection the Servant was also assured He would fulfill God's covenant promises to Israel and also be a light of promise for the Gentiles. And that one day there will be a glorious kingdom, and God will bring justice to the nations. (Isaiah 42:1) Jesus is the light of the world (John 8:12), and that includes the Gentiles!

We too are called to share the gospel of Jesus Christ with the world. God has given us the Holy Spirit to empower us to share His gospel message with all He brings across our path. We are both called and empowered to share the gospel. Unless we obey by living out what we know is truth, we are not fulfilling our part of God's plan in His bigger story.

Daily Bible reading
Isaiah 42:5-9
John 8:12

Something to think about

The days following Christmas, with all the lights of the season still shining all around us, is still a good time to share with those who haven't yet heard. In fact, every day is a good day to share the gospel. Use the coming New Year celebrations to open conversations about what their plans for the New Year are, as a segue to talk about making resolutions to lead into sharing the gospel.

It is important for each of us to determine now to prepare for and be alert to the opportunities all around us in the days ahead. It can be intimidating at first but be courageous, purpose to take the first step and God will pour out His grace enabling you to share. Each time you do, you will become more and more confident.

In order to be prepared to reflect God's grace to others pray and ask God to:
- Open your eyes to opportunities to share the gospel with those around you. As God opens the door, walk through it and share the gospel. (You may want to write the stories of those experiences in your journal pages. For example, HOW God opened the door, WHERE He opened it, WHO it was opened for and HOW they responded.)
- Give you names of people to share the gospel with. (Write down their names.) Then pray for each name on your list until they come to faith.

Hopefully you didn't simply read the entry for each day of the Advent season, but you journaled what the Lord revealed to you, each day on the pages provided. Now that you have completed the Advent season write those details you may have missed in years past: what captivated your heart this year, how this year impacts the way you will celebrate in years to come!

It has been my prayer that as the story unfolded before you, it recaptured your heart, connected the dots and restored that childlike, hope-filled wonder of Christmas! May you enter the New Year with a renewed understanding of the Hope that is yours in Jesus Christ!

ANNUAL ADVENT ASSESSMENT

At the end of each Advent season make a final journal entry of
- The year.
- What captivated your heart this year.
- How this year impacted the way you will celebrate in years to come.

Use it in following years to share at the beginning of the new Advent season as a way of remembering what God has said and done for you and your family.

Year _____

Annual Advent Assessment

Jesus' Names and Character Traits